From Wagons to Wings

Harry Arnold

All scripture is from the *King James Version* of the Bible.

From Wagons to Wings
By Harry Arnold

Copyright © 2016 by Harry Arnold
All Rights Reserved

ISBN: 978-0-9980622-0-4

Published by Harry Arnold | West Grove, PA 19390

Editorial by Jordan Media Services | P.O. Box 761593 | Fort Worth, Texas USA
www.jordanmediaservices.com

Typesetting/Layout by Ken Fraser | grafxedge@gmail.com | impactbookdesigns.com

Printed in the United States of America

Contents and/or cover may not be reproduced in whole or part in any form, stored in a retrieval system, or transmitted in any form by any means without the express written permission of the author/publisher, except as provided by United States of America copyright law.

Contents

Dedication
Prologue: The Relationship Between Mother and Son
Pre-Flight

Part One

Chapter 1: The Early Years 17
Flight Log: Takeoff 29
Chapter 2: A Death in the Family 33
Flight Log: Leveling Off 39
Chapter 3: A Change of Scenery 41
Flight Log: This Side of the Tracks 51
Chapter 4: Wagon Boys 53
Flight Log: Mid-Atlantic 61

Part Two

Chapter 5: Separation 65
Flight Log: The Other Side of the Tracks 77
Chapter 6: Working for Uncle Sam 81
Flight Log: Approaching the United States 91
Chapter 7: Wings 93
Flight Log: The Descent 103
Chapter 8: The Airlines: Part 1 105
Flight Log: Changing Landscape 117
Chapter 9: The Airlines: Part 2 121
Flight Log: Approach and Landing 133
Chapter 10: Post-Flight 139

Dedication

I dedicate this book to a number of people who have each played a very integral part in my life, and everything that I am.

Firstly, to my birth mother, Charlita Pembleton, and to my adoptive mother, Luebirda Arnold. They departed my life and this world too soon, but each left a lasting impression on me.

Secondly, to my dear brother, Cornelius Arnold—the one constant throughout my entire life. You have always been there for me—during my good times, and the difficult.

And thirdly, to my daughter, Camille Elisabeth Wilder, and my son, Corben Eugene Arnold. Thank you for making me proud to be called "Dad." I love you both dearly!

A final dedication goes my precious wife, Christine. She first encouraged me to write this book nearly 10 years ago, and she never stopping gnawing at me until I got busy. And today, mostly because of her persistence, I have completed what has been a lifelong desire. I love you, Christine, and I thank God for you every day.

Although my dedications are directed to these five people, to whom I am grateful and will always love dearly, I am also dedicating this book to someone else: My firstborn grandchild, Harrison James Wilder, and to any other grandchildren who may come behind him.

This book is the culmination of 10 years of research of legal documents, conversations with family and friends, and some deep soul-searching into my inner thoughts. During that time, I found many answers—some to questions I asked, and some to questions I never thought to ask. I tried to enter this journey with an open mind and a focus toward discovering and sharing the truth. Along the way, I realized the truth doesn't always provide the answers you really want to hear.

But the truth is the truth.

There were some things I discovered that are not included here. My desire is not to show anyone in a bad light, but to pass on to my children information they can someday share with their children—my descendants. I choose to do that here so that it won't be lost forever.

Camille and Corben are part of my legacy. They hold the keys to my vision for my descendants. I can picture my grandchildren someday approaching their parents and posing the question: "Who was my Papa and what was he like?" Knowing the personalities of Camille and Corben, I can imagine their response will be something like this: "Read the book, and then we will talk."

Prologue

The Relationship Between Mother and Son

How much bearing does the strength of a relationship between a mother and her young son have on the overall success of the son as he grows and develops into manhood? I believe that a sincere bonding during the early years goes a long way toward promoting emotional maturity and a sensitivity to issues in life for the son as he grows older. Respect for his mother builds a foundation that helps him develop as a husband and a father. This bonding process between a son and his mother facilitates communication between the future husband and his wife—the one thing that is most important in marriage. Lack of communication skills is one of the leading areas of weakness between a husband and wife.

But what happens when that bonding process is tragically disrupted by the untimely death of the mother when the son is 6 years old? How does he cope with the loss, especially when his mother was the only parent in a single-parent household? What happens when this loss is followed by several years of instability in the son's life because of unstable living conditions? What are the long-term consequences if these highly emotional issues are never addressed? Left unresolved, can these issues be addressed later in life, or do they leave scars and cause irreparable damage?

On the morning of his mother's death, the son had made her a promise. Years later, when his life seems to have some semblance of stability, he makes another promise—this one to his newly adoptive mother.

With two promises yet to be fulfilled, years go by. Unexpected events occur that jeopardize the fulfillment of either promise. Finally, the son makes yet a third promise—this one to himself. And for the next 30 years, this promise will be a guiding force in his life.

What were the promises the son made to his birth mother, his adoptive mother and to himself? Were they ever fulfilled?

Take your seat, fasten your seat belt, and prepare to take an insightful journey. Come aboard this flight and soar, with the son, through life. Ride along as he presses to keep his word and fulfill the promises he made—all because of his commitment to the belief that failure is never an option.

That's where you'll find the answers.

Pre-Flight

Saturday, Nov. 5, 2005, 8 A.M.
London Gatwick International Airport; London, England

Preparing an aircraft for an international flight requires a lot of people working together: the maintenance personnel, caterers, ground crew, flight dispatchers, gate agents, baggage handlers, flight attendants, and last but not least—the pilots! Most of these flights are considered routine, and are accomplished without disruption. In fact, pilots who fly international have jokingly referred to them as being 99 percent boredom and 1 percent stark terror.

But this is not your ordinary flight. Neither is the crew the typical flight crew.

I, an African American, sit at the helm of the aircraft as captain. My co-pilot and first officer is a white female. The diversity in the makeup of the flight crew is quite a change from what I experienced nearly 30 years ago when I first began my career with Continental Airlines.

Today's flight is my retirement flight.

Tomorrow I turn 60, the mandatory retirement age for pilots who fly for any commercial airline based in the United States.

Today's flight is the final segment of a three-day trip that started two days ago with Continental Airlines Flight 18 flying from Newark International Airport in New Jersey, to London Gatwick International Airport. Gatwick Airport is the United Kingdom's second largest airport and the busiest single-use runway airport in the world. It is located 28 miles south of London.

Accompanying me on this flight are 13 of my family members, a close friend from college and his wife.

The flight from Newark departed at 7 p.m. on Thursday, and arrived six and one-half hours later in London—early Friday morning. After clearing customs and checking into our rooms at the Gatwick Airport Hilton Hotel, we all rested for about three hours, then met in the hotel lobby to begin a day of sightseeing. We took the Gatwick Express train to downtown London, something I had done a number of times, then divided into several small groups to go sightseeing, shopping and taking a ride on the Tube, London's subway system.

We reassembled in the early evening for dinner at a restaurant my college buddy had preselected, based on his internet skills and his taste for fine foods. Some ended the evening with a nightcap back at the hotel before retiring. I passed, choosing instead to retire for the evening to get my "beauty sleep."

Headed Home!

Today, Continental Airlines Flight 19 from Gatwick International Airport to Newark International Airport is scheduled to depart London at 10:30 a.m. We're headed home.

I had asked my first officer to meet me in the Flight Operations weather room at 9 a.m. The Gatwick main terminal, train station and hotel are all interconnected. At 8:45 a.m., I check out of my hotel room and take the short walk from the hotel, past the train station and into the main airport terminal. Once there, I proceed past the small vendor shops to the far side of the terminal, and take the elevator to the sixth floor where flight operations are located.

As I proceed across the terminal toward the elevators, I notice several armed security personnel monitoring the movement of the passengers in the terminal. This sight has become common at most international airports since the tragic events that took place in New York City on September 11, 2001. The terrorist attacks on New York's World Trade Center, as well as the Pentagon, changed the lives of many forever. They also had a profound effect on the entire airline industry. I can recall, for instance, that one of my first flights following 9/11 was a two-day trip from Newark to London. On the second day of the trip, as I was completing my airplane exterior inspection in preparation for the return flight, I was approached by a British ground person who was loading baggage onto the aircraft. After we exchanged greetings, the man told me the British were behind the United States all the way. After a parting handshake, I couldn't shake that brief encounter which, even to this day, still has an effect on me. Thinking back, perhaps that single encounter was the reason London is one of my favorite cities. I've always loved the city's rich history and its present-day cosmopolitan flavor.

Upon exiting the sixth-floor elevator, I pass through two security checkpoints before entering the flight operations weather room. Once inside, I pause to take in the panoramic view of the Gatwick Airport taxiways and runway. Gazing across the airport grounds, I feel a lump rise in my throat as I see my aircraft being towed to Gate 15. A flood of mixed emotions fills me as I looked down on the Boeing 777-200 ER, tail number 001. She is a beautiful airplane. I love flying that "Triple Seven" aircraft.

Today's scheduled flight time back to Newark is just under seven hours, less than half the time of my regular trip series from Newark to Beijing, China. I would have preferred to fly my retirement flight to Beijing, but the challenge of coordinating the logistics of a travelling party of 15 to Beijing would have been difficult.

I smile as I think about my wife rounding up everyone at the hotel, leading them to the terminal, getting them through security, ushering them past the duty-free shops, and finally steering them to the departure gate. I ponder the difference in our personalities. Whereas I am more reserved and laid back, Christine is energetic and outgoing. With her beauty, personality and organizational skills, she possesses all the necessary qualities to be the perfect social director for all the activities surrounding my retirement flight.

For the past two months, she had worked tirelessly with the Continental Airlines Newark-based pilot office to make the arrangements for hotel rooms in Newark and London for the traveling party. She also made hotel arrangements for relatives and friends who are meeting us back in Newark for a retirement party this evening that has been planned for me. She did this despite the fact that, deep down inside, she is still grieving the loss of her mother, who passed three months ago at age 92.

Upon entering the operations room, I notice my first officer is already reading over the flight plan and other paperwork pertaining to our flight. This was no surprise, as she has always been conscientious, and very thorough. She is an excellent first officer and will someday be an excellent captain. As she reviewed the flight plan, she highlighted sections she felt would be important to me, including time en route, fuel requirements, weather reports, en route and arrival alternate airports, and any maintenance concerns. After reviewing the flight plan, she gives the paperwork to me, then turns her attention to plotting our route on a North Atlantic plotting chart.

In past years, the plotting chart was fairly important to the flight crew when aircrafts were using inertial navigation systems (INS) to navigate across the Atlantic Ocean. With the advent of the Global Positioning System (GPS), however, the plotting chart has mainly served as a backup.

After insuring the paperwork is in order and signing the dispatch release, we head downstairs, where we join other crew members passing through airport security, then head toward our departure gate.

When we arrive at Gate No. 15, the agent there informs me that my traveling party has cleared security and are already on their way to the gate. As I proceed through the waiting area to the jetway door, a few passengers give me a smile or a nod. I wonder if they know this is my retirement flight.

There is only one jetway, and it is connected to the midcabin door of the Boeing 777. As the first officer and I enter the aircraft cabin, we observe the flight attendants busy with their preflight checks. We continue on to the flight deck to store our flight and overnight bags, then undergo our initial cockpit safety checklist. With the checklist completed, the first officer proceeds to the tarmac, where she performs preflight inspection of the exterior of the aircraft.

When she returns to the flight deck, I ask the lead flight attendant to assemble her crew in first class for a briefing. The cabin crew is composed of a mixture of junior and middle-seniority international flight attendants. They have been very attentive to the needs of my traveling party on the flight from Newark to London. After I complete my crew briefing, the first officer and I return to the flight deck to commence our cockpit preflight aircraft checks. Looking out through the large windows of the flight deck, I suddenly become a little reflective in my thoughts. Sensing I want to be alone for a moment, my first office remains silent.

The silence is broken when the lead flight attendant leans in through the flight deck door to say my wife wants to come to the flight deck. Moments later, Christine joins us. Her presence always brightens my day. As she greets the first officer, she turns to her "Sweetie," to say that everyone is seated and comfortable. After a brief conversation, she squeezes my hand and returns to her seat.

After Christine leaves, I begin to reflect on each person in our traveling party. This flight is special to each of them, but it is even more special to one person in particular. This individual has been a constant for me my entire life. Without him, I may not have chosen the career path that eventually led to my becoming a pilot. This flight is the first he's ever flown with me.

I'm talking about my older brother.

Tomorrow, the two of us will have been siblings for 60 years.

The lead flight attendant comes to the flight deck to give me the final passenger count. There are 270 passengers, 12 flight attendants and the two pilots—a total of 284 SOB (Souls on Board). After she leaves the deck, I lock the flight deck door, turn to the first officer and say, "It's time to get this show on the road!"

Part 1

Chapter 1

The Early Years

My maternal grandmother, Idella Clay, was born in 1887 in Rosefield, Louisiana. The town of Rosefield is located in Catahoula Parish, midway between Monroe to the north and Alexandria to the south.

She had one brother and one sister from her mother's first marriage. When her mother later remarried, Idella got another brother and four more sisters. As she grew older, her siblings dropped the "I" from her name and began calling her "Della."

In the early part of the 20th century, Della moved several miles away from home and settled in the town of Standard, Louisiana, in LaSalle Parish. It was there that she met and married Champ Berryman. They had two children: a son named Frank and a daughter named Rattie. Della and Champ divorced after a several years of marriage, and Della married for a third time—this time to a man named Cleveland Pembleton.

Between 1910 to 1917, Cleveland and Della had four daughters: Luebirda, Ethel, Leola and Pauline. Cleveland died shortly after Pauline was born. Though it's not clear whether Della married for a fourth time, she gave birth to two more daughters: Helen Donald, in 1918; and Charlita Cross in 1921. Charlita later assumed the last name of Pembleton.

During the late 1920s and early 1930s, Della's children started leaving home. Frank, Luebirda and Helen moved to Omaha, Nebraska; and Pauline relocated to St. Louis,

Missouri. Rattie, Ethel and Leola moved away from home but remained in the area, leaving Charlita, the youngest daughter, the only child still living at home.

In 1940, at age 19, Charlita gave birth to a son and named him Bobby Lawrence. After his birth, Charlita went to work as a housekeeper for a prominent white family in Olla, Louisiana, about four miles south of Standard. She lived in a boarding house commonly referred to as "the long house." That's because the structure was literally one long building that contained five rooms, connected horizontally. Each room shared a common front porch, but had a separate entry and back door. Each room was occupied by an individual family, which sometimes numbered as many as five people.

Another name for the "long house" was the "shotgun" house, so-called because the rooms in each house were literally constructed with a clear pathway from the front to the rear. You could literally stand at the front door and see straight through to the back door. It was said that if someone stood at the front door and fired a shotgun, the pellets would travel straight through the house and out the back door without ever touching anything inside the house. The long house where Charlita lived was near Olla's main street and within walking distance to work.

Olla was a town of only about 1,000. It had a drugstore, post office, clothing store, grocery store, dry-goods store, gas station and movie theater. Most of the people from the surrounding towns conducted their business in Olla. About 95 percent of the population was white, and the remaining five percent was colored (black). Most of the black people in the area lived in nearby Standard.

Railroad tracks ran north to south through the middle of town, and separated the dry-goods store from the other stores. Two main roads crossed in the center of town. Louisiana Route 127 ran from southeast to northwest and Route 125 ran from south to north.

The main employers of the residents living in Olla were

two small lumber mills: Urania Lumber Company, which was about four miles to the south, and the Louisiana Central Lumber Company, located four miles to the north in Standard.

When Charlita moved to Olla, she left Bobby to live with his Grandma Della in Standard. When she was not working on the weekends, she would return to Standard so she could spend time with her son and her mother.

A year after moving to Olla, Charlita met a man named Lonnie Tatum. Lonnie had recently moved to Olla from Arkansas to be near his brother, Jeff.

Jeff, who lived only a short distance from where Charlita stayed in the long house, was a truck driver and hauled lumber for one of the local sawmills. He also was the barber for most, if not all, the black men in the area.

Working two jobs was pretty common back then, especially among blacks.

Lonnie Tatum, for instance, drove a truck for a milling company but also worked at the local gas station. During the rainy season, when the pulp-wood trucks couldn't get back into the tree-cutting areas of the forest because of muddy roads, there was no work for the drivers. That meant drivers didn't get paid. Having a second job to fall back on meant they would at least have some income.

Not long after Lonnie's arrival in Olla, he and Charlita struck up a relationship and Lonnie moved in with her. Their first child, a boy they named Arnold, was born February 1943. Two years later, in November 1945, a second child, Lonnie Tatum Jr., was born.

Lonnie Tatum Jr.

That was my birth name.

Arnold and I took on my father's last name. But my mother, Charlita, remained Pembleton since she and Lonnie weren't married.

My mother's daily work routine often differed, but always began with her leaving home to make breakfast for the white family she worked for. Some days, if there was no house-cleaning to do, she would return home, then go back in the afternoons to fix dinner. Other days, when there was cleaning and laundry to do, she would remain there until evening. In her absence, Arnold and I were left in the care of my mother's niece, Jean, the second eldest of my Aunt Leola. Jean was just a few years older than Arnold.

I can remember when things started to get bad between my mom and dad. I'm not real sure, but it's possible that there was tension between them because of the crowded conditions in our shotgun row house. But more than likely, it was because my father would stay out all hours of the night. I just remember that when he would return home, they argued.

As time passed, things got worse. My father got to the point where he only came home to change clothes and was gone again. Eventually, my mother took Arnold and me and moved to another shotgun house a distance up the road, across the street from where my father's brother, Jeff, lived. As my father became more and more distant in his relationship with my mother, she pretty much became the sole support for the three of us. I may not have known it then, but the truth is, we were poor. I suppose it just never registered with me because my mother poured out so much love to my brother and me. And we loved her. Though Arnold and I didn't understand why our father was never there, it didn't affect the bond that had been created among the three of us.

I have many fond memories of my early years, like when I turned 2, and Aunt Ethel gave me a peppermint candy stick. I devoured that candy stick in record time. So quickly, in fact, that Aunt Ethel started calling me "Candy." The nickname stuck with me even into my adult years.

My whole world was centered on my mother and my older brother. Arnold and I were playmates during the day, and at night we slept in a small bed with our mother. We also grew very fond of Jean during that time, since she was always our babysitter when mother had to be away for work or attending some social event.

I also have strong memories of being educated to something called Jim Crow, the segregation laws that existed in Olla, and the South in general. This was especially the case when I would accompany my mother into town. The white people were allowed to enter business establishments through the front entrance, but blacks could only enter through the side or rear doors. I became starkly aware of that practice one day when I was in the drugstore. I was standing next to a parrot that belonged to someone in the store, when suddenly I heard the parrot say the word *nigger*.

When I was 3 years old, my brother Arnie and I got our first summer job—picking wild blackberries. It was something we wanted to do because we thought it was a lucrative endeavor. Imagine being 3 and already deciding what was profitable. Turns out there was a drawback.

Snakes would slither underneath the blackberry bushes, either to cool off from the midday sun or to nest their litter. A young boy with no shoes, and wearing bib overalls that were too short and had holes in the knees, made a very inviting target for any snake. To say I was afraid of snakes would be a gross understatement. I always made it a point to throughly inspect a bush before picking blackberries. Even then, I kept an eye out for the crawling intruders.

On one particular occasion, Arnie and I were picking blackberries when I spied a large snake under the bush. I warned Arnie, but he went right on picking because that particular bush was loaded with berries. Needless to say, abundance or not, I was done picking from that bush. I moved to a nearby tree and waited for Arnie to finish. When he came over to where I was standing a few minutes later, I asked him if he had seen the snake and he said no. Years later, however, Arnie came clean and told me he had seen the snake that day. He also said that from that time on, and unbeknownst to me, he let me choose the bushes we picked from.

If we were fortunate enough to collect a gallon bucket of berries, we could sell them to a white family for 50 cents. If we were really lucky and came across a bush early enough in the day that was loaded with blackberries, we could pick a bucket to sell and still have time to pick at least another half bucket to take home. If our mother wasn't too tired after work, she would make us a blackberry pie. If she didn't feel up to making a pie, she would mix some of the berries with milk and sugar to create blackberry floats—without the ice cream.

Another summer adventure had my brother and me fishing for crawfish in the creek near our house. To catch the crawfish, we would tie a small piece of salt pork to a piece of string about 5 feet long. Then, we would tie the other end of the string to a small stick that served as our fishing pole. We would lower the salt pork into the clear water of the creek and place it about an inch from the crawfish, which nested on the creek bottom. Once the crawfish began to nibble the meat, we would snatch it up from the water. Once on the creek bank, the crawfish became the first ingredient for a nice pot of crawfish etouffee.

At least one or two days a week during the summer, Arnie and I would walk the four miles to Standard and spend the day with our brother, Bobby, and Grandma Della. If we wanted to spend the night, we would have to get permission from our mother before she left for work in the morning.

Grandma Della lived on a quarter-acre lot in Standard. Her home was the gathering place for all the children and grandchildren, especially on Sundays and for holidays. She grew most of her own vegetables in her garden, and also had several fruit trees. She also had one rooster and several chickens. Actually, one rooster was all she needed. The chickens were a source for fresh eggs and the occasional fried-chicken dinner. My favorite fruit tree was the plum tree. My brothers and I would get up early each morning during fruit harvesting season and race to the plum tree in search of the best-looking plum on the tree.

If Arnie and I spent a couple of days at Grandma Della's, Arnie, Bobby and I would get up early on one of those days and walk to our Uncle Selma and Aunt Leola Kavanaugh's house in Kelly. Kelly was about five miles north of Standard. We would spend the day playing with our cousins. At that time, Uncle Selma and Aunt Leola had five children, including Jean, our babysitter. My brothers and I would spend most of our time playing with our cousins: Clynnis, who we called "Bubba," and Wren. Thinking back, there must be at least one person named "Bubba" in every family from the South.

Even though Aunt Leola had a lot of mouths to feed, she would ensure that there was enough food to feed all the children lunch. Arnie and I enjoyed spending time with our relatives, but returning home to see our mom again was always a treat.

In the town of Olla, Friday and Saturday nights were the main nights for attending the movie theater. There was one movie theater in Olla, and the seating arrangements for blacks and whites were further evidence of Jim Crow laws being in full effect. The whites were allowed to sit on the main level of the theater, while blacks had to sit in the balcony. To get to the balcony, blacks would enter the theater through a side door, purchase their tickets at a side window, then climb the stairs to the balcony. This process was not visible to the white patrons, who entered through the front door on the main level.

If blacks wanted to buy popcorn or candy, they had to descend the same stairs leading to the balcony and make their purchase at the same side window where they bought their tickets. Often, they had to wait until an attendant was finished serving the white patrons and made the time to serve them. The blacks drank from a water faucet that was located outside the theater.

Sometimes, if blacks didn't have enough money to buy a ticket, they would try to sneak into the theater while the movie attendant was serving the white patrons in the main lobby. The only drawback was that occasionally the ticket agent would come to the balcony and check for ticket stubs. It you got caught without a ticket stub, you would have to leave. If you were lucky, someone holding a ticket would slip you theirs so you didn't get thrown out of the theater. Otherwise, you were victim to the theater's rule: "No stub, no stay!"

After attending a movie, the walk home usually turned into an adventure. Lights lined the main streets in Olla, but the road leading to my house had no lights. The farther I got away from the main streets, the darker it became. As I proceeded through total darkness, I would sometimes have to stop walking until my eyes adjusted to the dark. Those few moments of adjustment sometimes seemed like an eternity.

Saturday was usually haircut day. Since my Uncle Jeff was the local barber for all the blacks in the Olla area, he spent most of the day cutting hair. He would schedule appointments for the adults and squeeze in time for the children between appointments.

On Sundays I would get up early, dress for church and walk with my mother and brother to Standard to attend Star Light Baptist Church. The church was located at the end of a road that ran alongside Grandma Della's house.

Going to church on Sundays was an all-day affair. My brothers and I attended Sunday school while our mother visited with Grandma Della and any other of our relatives who were attending church on that particular Sunday. After Sunday school, the adults and children would all attend the main service and afterward we gathered at Grandma Della's house for a big meal. The children weren't allowed to do much playing because we were wearing our Sunday dress clothes and would be returning to church later in the evening. After the evening service, my mother, Arnie and I would return to Olla. Sometimes, during the summer months, Arnie and I would remain in Standard and spend a couple of days with Grandma Della.

Early School Days

I entered grade school in the fall of 1950. Arnie had started school the previous year. Because Jim Crow laws dictated the segregation of the public schools, we could not attend elementary school in Olla. Instead, we were bused 22 miles away to the Good Pine grade school/high school, just outside the city of Jena. Good Pine was the designated school for all black students, first grade through high school, who lived in the Olla, Standard and Jena areas.

I remember those days well. Each morning the driver, Mr. Payton, would drive up in a big, yellow school bus as we all waited outside the Olla Drug Store. Then, he would drive north along Route 125 to pick up other students in Standard. There were more black students in the Standard area than in Olla. With his bus loaded, Mr. Payton would preceed on to Jena. For those of us living in Olla, that meant an hour-long bus ride to Good Pine School.

As the bus turned onto the school grounds, Arnie gave me instructions for where things were located (so I wouldn't get lost on my first day). The grade school was on my right, and the cafeteria was inside the building to my left. The administration building, where the principal's office was located, was in the center of the school grounds. And behind the administration building was the school's athletic field. Other incidentals included the dirt-covered basketball courts, located near the high school building, and, of course, the girls' and boys' outhouses, which were on the far end of the school grounds.

Polio vaccinations were of major importance during the early 1950s, so all new students at Good Pine were required to get vaccinated by the school nurse on the first day of orientation. Standing in a long line, and listening as other students screamed to the top of their lungs as they were getting shots, wasn't exactly how I pictured spending my first day of school.

Although I was probably among the poorest students in my class, I quickly adapted to my new environment and did very well in school. My favorite subject was math, at which I quickly excelled. My second favorite was lunchtime, followed closely by recess. At lunch, the high school students received preferential treatment, being allowed to eat before the other students. Next were the middle, or upper-grade students, and then those in the lower grades. That was my class.

Back then, lunch cost only 10 cents. Each day my mother would give me 15 cents—a dime for lunch and 5 cents to spend however I chose.

My favorite game during recess was marbles. Over time I became pretty good, and often, at the end of a school day I would have a pocket full of marbles that I had won playing with the other students. I became so good at shooting marbles, in fact, that eventually the kids my age refused to play against me, so I started playing with the older students. They say looks can be deceiving, and as a small kid I certainly proved that to be a true saying. When I would ask the older guys if I could shoot marbles with them, they looked at me, a small kid dressed in ragged clothes, and considered that I would be easy prey. Most of the time, though, I got the last laugh because at the end of the day I would walk away with all my marbles, and most of theirs.

Most often, I would save my extra 5 cents for the bus ride home after school. If the kids were not loud and unruly, Mr. Payton would sometimes reward us by stopping at a Dairy Queen, where I would buy myself an ice cream cone. Sometimes, the kids would start to act up after we stopped at Dairy Queen. But Mr. Payton had a remedy for that. On the ride home the next day, no matter how well-mannered and behaved we were, he would drive right pass Dairy Queen and keep on going!

I always wondered where Mr. Payton lived, but never really knew. I thought he may have lived in nearby Urania, and that he drove the bus to his home each day after dropping off the last students in Olla. Or maybe he live in Jena, near where the school was, and made the return trip each day after letting us off in front of the drugstore. If I were to hazard a guess, I would say he lived in Urania.

First grade went by fast, and I did really well in all my

classes. That summer, Arnie and I returned to our summer activities of picking wild blackberries, fishing for crawfish, spending time with relatives, and swimming in the pond near Grandma Della's house—the same pool the church used for baptism.

We still found time to get in an occasional fight with the kids who lived in the long house. I looked forward to the end of summer and the beginning of my second-grade year at Good Pine. In second grade, I discovered a much better use for the extra 5 cents my mother gave me for lunch each day.

It was during second grade that I first experienced what the older folks so kindly referred to as "puppy love." The target was a girl in my class named Gracie. She had the prettiest eyes I had ever seen. In those days, people referred to them as "cat eyes."

I was smitten by Gracie from the first time I saw her, even though I felt there was very little chance of her being attracted to me, especially with me being a poor person. Still, occasionally I would offer my extra nickel to Gracie and she would accept it. After a while, I learned that Gracie was attracted to a boy in my class who lived in the Jena area, where she lived.

I guess you could say from that came my first real lesson regarding romance. First, I learned to never give my 5 cents (or 2 cents, for that matter) to a female; and second, I quickly discovered that a long-distance relationship is a difficult thing to maintain.

Lessons learned!

Change Is on the Horizon

During the summer of 1952, I gave my heart to the Lord and joined Star Light Baptist Church. I was baptized in the same pond where my friends and I went often to swim. Some of the older kids earned money by picking cotton in the cotton fields, something Arnie and I were still too young to do, so we continued to pick blackberries to make money.

At 8 a.m. on Saturday, August 9, 1952, my mother left home for work. Saturday was usually not a workday for her, and normally she would spend the time with Arnie and me. But on this day, she had decided to work to earn a little extra money.

I always looked forward to spending time with our mother on the weekends. She had told us she would only be working a few hours that day and promised to do something special with us when she returned home from work around noon. Her instructions to us before leaving were the same as always: "Arnie watch out for your little brother. Candy, stay close to your big brother."

We both replied, almost in unison: "Yes, ma'am."

After our mother left the house, Arnie and I went to play down by the creek. At around 11 o'clock we went and sat on the fence near our house to wait for mother to return. It was our habit that, when we saw her coming, we would jump from the fence and run and greet her. Each of us would grab a leg, squeeze it tightly, and then ask if she had bought anything for us. Sometimes, mother would stop off at the store and buy us candy. Or, she would have something that her employer had given her to bring to us.

Before long, it was noon. And we had not seen our mother.

Then, it happened.

As Arnie and I sat perched atop the fence, we saw the parish sheriff approaching in his car and park in front of Uncle Jeff's house. Moments later, Uncle Jeff came outside and the two of them began to talk while glancing over at Arnie and me.

Suddenly, we saw somebody running toward us, screaming and yelling as he came. At first, we didn't recognize who it was or understand what he was saying. As he came closer, we recognized it was Bobby, our older brother.

We also heard clearly the words he yelled:

"Mom is dead!"

Flight Log: Takeoff

Once the flight deck door is locked and secured, I call for the "before pushback, before start" checklist. Pushback is a procedure during which an aircraft is pushed backward away from the gate in preparation for takeoff.

Because another aircraft is parked in the alleyway behind our plane, ground control says there will be a slight delay before we can receive pushback clearance. When the aircraft is clear, I inform the pushback crew and in short order the plane begins moving backward. As I look up at the windows in the terminal building, I can see several of Continental's gate agents waving goodbye. I smile as I wave back.

As the pushback crew maneuvers our aircraft around so that it faces the outbound taxiway, we notice there are firetrucks positioned along each side.

For years, water salutes have been used to mark such notable events as the retirement of a senior pilot or air traffic controller, the first or last flight of an airline to an airport, or the first or last flight of a type of aircraft. Traditionally, a vehicle travels under plumes of water that are expelled by one or more vehicles. I expected that, likely, there would be a water salute waiting for me in Newark, but had not even given thought to one being planned as part of my final London departure.

Once pushback is completed, I set the parking brake and inform the pushback crew that they are clear to disconnect the tug from the aircraft. One ground crewman will remain in contact with me until both engines are started. I smile as the left engine roars to life. There's just something special about the sound of those CFM engines. After starting the second engine, I clear the ground crewman to disconnect and tell him, "Have a good day!"

He replies: "Enjoy your retirement!"

Rejoining the first officer on the No. 1 VHF radio, she gives me the "after engine start" checklist. I request taxi clearance from ground control and proceed to runway 26L. I flash the aircraft's nose taxi light to signal the ground crewman that we have received clearance, then gently begin moving the throttles forward. As the Boeing 777 slowly moves forward, the lead ground crewman steps off to the side and joins the other members of the pushback crew. In unison, they all honor me with a salute. Smiling, I return their salute. I think, *Those Brits really know how to do things well.*

As the plane taxies between the two firetrucks, the firemen turn on their hoses, sending a burst of water over the top of the aircraft. As the aircraft continues to taxi, those onboard begin snapping pictures. It's a beautiful sight!

Amid the celebration, and having completed another checklist, we taxi to runway 26L, lining up behind a British Airways 747 that is about to take off. As we ready ourselves for takeoff, another aircraft is about to land. After it lands, the control tower clears us into position on the runway. While calling to the first office for the "before takeoff" checklist, I increase the power to taxi onto the runway—getting in position for takeoff. Once cleared for takeoff, I turn on my landing lights to signal the other aircraft I'm about to commence my takeoff roll, then move the throttles into takeoff power setting. As the throttles reached midrange position, and became fully engaged, I call for the first officer to check to make sure they are at the correct power setting.

Today, the aircraft weighs only 545,000 pounds, well below the maximum takeoff weight of 648,000 pounds. That means acceleration is now much quicker.

There are a number of decisions that must be made, both prior to takeoff and once an aircraft is airborne. And while none of these are visible to the passengers, they are critical to the safety of the flight.

For instance, our V1 (or decision) speed today is 124 knots. Once the plane reaches this speed at takeoff, we are committed to continue takeoff—even if we encounter engine failure. There are several callouts and acknowledgements between the first officer and the captain during the takeoff process, as well as during landing.

When the first officer calls "V1," I immediately remove my hand from the throttles and place both hands on the yoke (control wheel). After passing V1, she calls out "rotate." I respond by easing back on the yoke at the rate of one and a half to two degrees per second toward a pitch attitude of 10 degrees. As the plane continues to accelerate, its nose wheel comes off the runway, followed by the main gears, as the aircraft transitions from a high-speed tricycle to a flying machine. With so many years of experience to back me up, I believe takeoff is the most critical time for the aircraft. The landing is the most critical time for the pilot.

Once the Boeing 777 clears the runway, and has a positive rate of climb, I call for the landing gear to be retracted. The Gatwick Tower controller instructs us to contact London Departure Control, then adds a personal touch by wishing me a happy retirement.

"Thanks, I'll do just that," I respond.

With a few minor adjustments, we level off at 10,000 feet and are on our way home. The flight will take us past Birmingham, over Cardiff, Wales; over the Irish Sea, across the southern portion of Ireland north of Limerick and then out over the Atlantic Ocean. As we approach Birmingham, I think for a moment about the many layovers I've had in that lovely city. The hotel where I stayed was rumored to have been haunted, but I never saw any ghosts. I wonder what Shakespeare would think about his old hometown.

As we maneuver the aircraft above 10,000 feet, I notify the flight attendants that the cockpit is no longer sterile, meaning they can contact the flight deck if necessary. As we fly over the Irish Sea, we exit London Center airspace and enter Shannon Domestic airspace. Soon we reach an altitude of 31,000 feet, and then level off at 34,000 feet. As we do, I suddenly have a sobering thought. I think about Arnold, and the promise I made to him so many years before.

Chapter 2

A Death in the Family

Death seems to ask some questions to which there are no immediate answers—especially true when it happens unexpectedly. It's also the case when there are young children involved, and it's the mother who has died. Aren't children supposed to experience long life with their parents? We cry out to God for answers, but the questions seem to never come. Or, they fall on deaf ears.

When I was finally able to hear clearly what Bobby was saying—that my mother was dead—my first instinct was to look to Arnie for an explanation. The only thing I got was a quizzical look. He didn't understand either.

My second instinct was to cry, but I didn't. At least not right way. For some reason, I held back my tears. Maybe, just maybe, Bobby had heard wrong. Maybe our mother was not dead. That's what I wanted to believe. That's what we all wanted to believe. But that was not to be. Bobby had heard correctly.

Our mother was dead.

As shock began to set in, I began to shut out everything and everyone. That moment had become real, and my young mind just could not comprehend what I was now facing.

Shock and Disbelief

As news of our mother's death quickly spread throughout

the community, the adults began to deal with their own disbelief. They also asked questions. How did it happen? Was her death an accident, or was it intentional? Who's going to explain this incident to her two young sons? Who's going to take care of the two boys?

For a while I wanted to lie down and fall asleep, thinking maybe when I woke up I would find it was all a dream. Even that thought raised questions for me. Questions like, where would I sleep that night? Would I even be able to sleep at all knowing my mother wasn't sleeping next to me?

We would soon learn that Grandma Della had all the answers, including how our mother had died. It was an accidental shooting, she said.

For the funeral, family came from near and far. Our aunts, Rattie, Leola and Ethel. all lived nearby. Aunt Luebirda, Aunt Helen, and Uncle Frank came from Omaha, Nebraska, and Aunt Pauline came from St. Louis, Missouri. Because there wasn't a black-owned funeral home in Olla, my mother's body was taken to Monroe, about 50 miles away. It was decided that Arnie and I would live with Grandma Della until more permanent arrangements could be made. The family would have to act quickly, or else we would become wards of the State of Louisiana.

Eventually, Grandma Della gave us more details about our mother's death.

The 16-year-old son of the family she worked for had been cleaning a shotgun, when the gun accidentally discharged. The blast apparently went through a wall and struck my mother in the back as she was standing at the kitchen sink washing dishes.

I don't know that I ever had any real reason to not believe that story. But for years following that tragic incident, I still had my doubts.

Even knowing what happened to my mother, and at least having the comfort of knowing the circumstances surrounding our future had been addressed and we would be staying with family, my emotional state was never fully addressed. I went through the physical motions of my daily activities, but emotionally I was still in a state of shock. I kept thinking that someday I would wake up from this terrible dream.

In all my six years on this earth, I had never attended a funeral. In some ways, there was a certain mystique that surrounded death and cemeteries that was scary. I wouldn't even venture near a graveyard during the day, let alone at nighttime.

On the day of my mother's funeral, the sky was clear and the temperature was in the 80s. It would have been a good day for her to take my brother and me to town after she finished work for the day. And, because it was Friday, she could have taken us to a movie that night. But this would not be the case. Reality was reality, and our mother was dead.

The funeral was held at Star Light Baptist Church, and was attended by both blacks and whites—something you didn't see too often in the 1950s. But even at that, the "Jim Crow" signs of segregation were very prevalent. Whites lined the south side of the road leading to the church, while blacks stood on the north side, awaiting the arrival of the hearse carrying our mother's body. We would later learn it was the first time so many blacks and whites had attended a funeral together in the history of Olla.

While standing with my brothers along the roadside, a white woman crossed the road and approached me. She had tears in her eyes, and told us she was very sorry about the death of our mother. I believed at the time that she might have been the mother of the boy who accidently shot our mother. Later, I learned I was right. I also found out the reason the boy was not at the funeral was that he was too distraught over the incident to attend.

The hearse finally arrived, and six pallbearers carried the casket into the church. With so many people in attendance, the church couldn't hold them all, and many were forced to stand outside. They didn't seem to mind, which obviously meant they thought well of my mother.

Grandma Della, my brothers and I were seated on the front row, near where the casket had been placed. When they opened the casket, suddenly it struck me that it was the first time I had seen my mother since she left home for work that Saturday morning. For some reason, she looked different. Her skin looked darker, and her frame smaller than I remembered. On most days, my mother kept her hair looking very nice. But lying there in that casket, her hair didn't look as well-kept.

It was then that the reality of what had happened, and what was going on even then, set in and I began to cry.

My mother was buried in Oak Forest Cemetery—the cemetery where all the blacks in the area were laid to rest. The graveside service was brief, probably because the minister was beginning to notice how fidgety my brothers and I were becoming. As I stood next to the casket, I overheard someone nearby whisper, "I wonder what is going to happen to those boys."

After the funeral service, Grandma Della asked that same question to her children. It was her intention to continue taking care of Bobby, but trying to raise three boys would for sure be too much for her, especially considering the fact that she suffered with high blood pressure.

It was clear that Aunt Leola, who already had five children of her own, couldn't take on two more. Plus, her oldest daughter, Scotia, had just married. Sending us to Omaha or St. Louis was out of the question. Subsequently, Arnie and I were shuffled between Grandma Della, our two aunts, and Scotia and her husband.

The start of the school year was rapidly approaching, and more permanent arrangements for Arnie and me had to be made very soon. For whatever reason, my father remained silent throughout the entire ordeal. Not once did he step up and say he would do the right thing and take care of his two sons. His brother, Jeff, finally opened his home to us and we went to live with him. Actually, it turned out to be a blessing for Arnie and me, and was really the best solution to the problem.

We moved in with Uncle Jeff just before the start of

school in the fall of 1952. Being back in school brought a sense of normalcy to my life, but there were times, lots of them, when I would have my moments, particularly when I returned home from school and saw my old house, which was directly across the street from where I now lived. The bottom line was that I had not gotten over losing my mother. I wouldn't—for a long, long time.

As time passed, Arnie and I grew even closer. We both were feeling the same pain, and we were both haunted by the same questions: Why did this happen to us? Why did God take away our mother? Were we such bad boys that no one wanted us? At one point, we began to feel a sense of abandonment and a loss of identity.

In August of that year, our Aunt Luebirda came for a visit and asked Arnie and me if we wanted to go back to Omaha, Nebraska, with her for a visit. She thought a change in the environment would be good for us. Or, at least that's what she told Uncle Jeff. Despite the fact that Arnie and I had begun to feel a bit more comfortable with our new arrangement, later that month we boarded a Greyhound bus with Aunt Luebirda for what was supposed to be a summer visit. Little did I know that the entire thing had been orchestrated. A plan had been hatched by Grandma Della and our aunts to get Arnie and me away from Olla—for good! Little did I know that, once I left, it would be 50 years before I would ever set foot back in Olla, Louisiana.

✈ Flight Log: Leveling Off

Continental 19 levels off at its final cruising altitude of 34,000 feet just as the aircraft is passing south of Dublin and north of Shannon, Ireland. Then, we prepare to cross over the Atlantic Ocean. We transmit a data link to the Shanwick Oceanic Control to confirm our route across the Atlantic. Shanwick is tasked with designing the westbound flight tracks, similar to highways, from Europe to North America. These tracks start at around 10 degrees west latitude and continue westbound until around 50 degrees latitude. Shanwick controls the air space from the 10-degree point west to 30 degrees west latitude, which is the midpoint of the track system. At 30 degrees, control is taken over by the Gander Oceanic Control Center in Gander, Newfoundland.

The westbound tracks are designated by letters, from A to G, and are separated laterally by 60 miles. Within each track, aircraft are separated 1,000 miles vertically, beginning at 29,000 feet and ending at 41,000 feet. To maintain an orderly flow on each track, each aircraft must maintain its assigned airspeed. If airspeed changes by more than 10 knots, or if there is the possibility that the plane will arrive at its checkpoint either three minutes early or late, the pilot is required to alert the controlling agency.

Generally, tracks C and D are the most desirable for winds. Also, the higher the altitude the better the fuel consumption for the aircraft. Gander Oceanic designs the eastbound flight tracks for aircraft that fly eastbound from North America to Europe. It uses the same criteria as Shanwick, but its tracks are defined by the letters T through Z.

Today, Continental 19 is scheduled for Track B at an altitude of 34,000 feet, which is our first choice, and Track C at 33,000 feet as a second choice. There is an excellent chance of us getting our first choice. It's very rare that an aircraft is given a different track from that which it initially requested. Also there is the possibility that an aircraft could be assigned the same filed track, but at a different altitude. This is not a major factor except that a different altitude may cause a higher fuel burn than what was originally planned.

Chapter 3

A Change of Scenery

The Greyhound bus pulled out of the small bus station in Olla and headed north on Route 125. The first major city we passed through was Monroe. For a moment, sadness overcame me as I reflected on my mother's death a year ago, and the thought that this was likely the same route the funeral procession took when her body was brought from Monroe to Olla for the funeral.

During the ride I had much to ponder.

What was Omaha like? When would I return to Olla?

During the past year I had become close to Uncle Jeff. I believed he really cared about Arnie and me. But despite that, there had always been a nagging thought that maybe we would do something to cause him to want to get rid of us.

Was that why we were being shipped off to Nebraska?

I tried to not think about it.

We all sat near the back of the bus. Arnie and I sat together, he next to the window and I in the aisle seat. Aunt Luebirda sat in the aisle seat directly across from me. It didn't mean anything to Arnie and me that, like all the other black passengers, we were sitting near the rear of the bus. But when the driver stopped in Shreveport to allow passengers to take a rest, things began to come clear to us when we noticed there were separate water fountains and seating areas for blacks and whites. Even though we had traveled a distance from the racist treatment that had been such a major part of living in Olla, it appeared nothing would be different where we were headed.

We would later come to learn that Jim Crow wasn't just exclusive to Olla and its surrounding areas. It was a big part of the South in those days.

The bus ride to Nebraska took about five days. Not because it was that long a drive, but because of stops we made along the way. First, there was the detour through Little Rock, Arkansas; and Memphis, Tennessee; to St. Louis, Missouri; where we stopped off to visit my Aunt Pauline and her family. I still have vivid memories of that visit, including the fact that it was the first time Arnie and I had ever seen indoor plumbing. We thought we had died and gone to heaven!

We also got to ride a taxicab for the first time.

After spending three days in St. Louis, we arrived in Omaha on Saturday, August 29, 1953.

Hello, Omaha!

It didn't take long to learn the logistics of Omaha, thanks to a savvy taxi driver who turned out to be a very gracious and obliging tour guide.

The Greyhound bus station was located in the center of Omaha, a block away from the Omaha Courthouse. All of the major department stores, theaters, hotels and office buildings were located in a 10 block square area called "downtown Omaha."

As we traveled along Dodge Street, the driver pointed out the former state capitol building, which had been converted into Central High School. He also pointed out that the famed Mutual of Omaha Building, Omaha University and Peony Park were also on Dodge Street.

The taxi turned off Dodge and onto 24th Street.

With the exception of Creighton University, a prominent Catholic school in the city, we were done seeing the elite sections of Omaha. Now we were entering a section of town known as the "near north side." It was an area with a heavy concentration of blacks, but also populated with a sprinkling of European immigrant, working-class whites. Riding along

North 24th Street, I saw a horde of blacks in the Kellum Grade School swimming pool. I remember wondering how it was possible for so many people to fit in one pool.

We rode through the black business district, and continued along 24th Street, most notably referred to by blacks in the area as "Chocolate Avenue." It was several more minutes before we reached our destination, but finally the driver steered the taxi into the small driveway of the house at 2875 Binney Street.

Finally, we were home.

The first thing that caught my eye was the large wagon wheel in the front yard. The spokes were painted white and the outer rim was painted red. I would soon learn that the wheel had become a prominent landmark in the community for directing people to our aunt and uncle's house.

The lawn was well-kept, as was the case with most homes in the area. There was a tall post with a streetlight in front of the house. I thought it surely would have been nice to have one of these lights in front of my house back in Olla, that night I was walking home from the theater.

Inside, a small entryway opened up to a family room. A door directly to the left of the main entrance led to the master bedroom. Inside the living room was a large sofa and console TV. Off the hallway to the left was a second bedroom, where Arnie and I would sleep. And then there was the bathroom—with indoor plumbing!

It was a really nice house!

This was the first time we had met Uncle Cornelius since he was not able to attend my mother's funeral. He was 14 years older than Aunt Luebirda, which didn't get my attention at all until I learned that he was born in 1897. That made him seem very old. We got a pretty quick history on Uncle Cornelius, including the fact that his grandfather had been a slave in the South, and that he only went as far as fourth grade before dropping out of school. Aunt Luebirda had dropped out of school after sixth grade. The two were married when she was 13 and he was 27.

When we came to live with them, Aunt Luebirda was 43 and Uncle Cornelius was 57. Friends and neighbors questioned why they would be so willing to take on two small children so late in life, but it didn't bother them. The truth is, they had tried to have children for years but were never able to. They both were pretty strong people, and nobody forced them to take Arnie and me, so I guess they figured they could handle raising us with no problems.

Our first day of school was on September 9. My head seemed to be spinning as I tried to digest everything that was taking place in my life: living in a new home and new neighborhood, new guardians, and a new school. One good thing, though, was the fact that Howard Kennedy Grade School was only about two minutes away from Aunt Luebirda's house. That was a welcome change, considering the 22-mile schoolbus ride we had endured the year before when we lived in Olla. With the school being so close, I was able to go home for lunch, and still have time to return to the playground before the afternoon session started.

I wondered if anyone played marbles at my new school.

Howard Kennedy had a good reputation in comparison with other grade schools in the Omaha area. The student body was made up of area children who lived in homes surrounding the school, mostly from the Spencer Street projects.

I don't know why I thought getting started with school would put further distance between me and the sad memories I had of my mother's passing. It didn't.

At registration the questions, which came like rocket blasts, took me right back to Olla.

Questions like, "What is your father's name?"

"Lonnie Tatum. He lives in Louisiana."

"What is your mother's name?"

"Her name is Charlita Pembleton, but she is deceased. I live with my aunt and uncle."

When I couldn't answer whether or not Aunt Luebirda and Uncle Cornelius were my legal guardians, the woman became so exasperated, she told me to stand off to the side of the line so she could register the other students. She would get back to me later, she said.

Though we didn't know it at the time, Arnie and I had also become the victims of culture shock. We spoke with a Southern drawl, and were considered by most as being "country bumpkins." That positioned us as perfect targets for being teased and bullied by some of the students. For instance, we quickly learned the art of "crowing." Crowing was when two students would engage in a verbal fight and try to outdo each other by picking at or pointing out flaws in the other student's character or clothing.

Here's an example of how a "crowing" contest between two students would go:

First student: "Your pants are so short it looks like you are preparing for a flood."

Second student: "You have some nice shoes. It's too bad you didn't take them out of the box before you wore them."

While the exchange was taking place, other students were standing around encouraging both students with cheers, jeers and laughter. When one of the competitors crossed the line, usually by saying something derogatory about the other student's mother or sister (I guess insults about dads and brothers didn't matter), it was almost inevitable that a physical fight would break out between the two.

From the very beginning Aunt Luebirda took an active role in our education, not just in school but also at home. She stressed the importance of education, as well as speaking properly. That's why she was quick to agree with our teacher that Arnie and I should enroll in a speech class. The first words out of a person's mouth always leave a lasting impression, she said.

I learned a lot from my Aunt Luebrida. Things like the importance of having "Mother's Wit," something black people used to describe wisdom or common sense. "There's nothing like an educated fool," she would sometimes say, describing people who have much education but never use common sense.

She also taught me about respect, especially regarding my elders. To this day, I don't mind going out of my way to assist elderly people when they need help.

Mrs. Winston, who was Aunt Luebirda's best friend and lived across the street from us, and Mrs. Pye, who lived next door to us, were both widows. Aunt Luebirda had made it clear that whenever Arnie and I mowed Mrs. Winston's lawn, we were expected to do the same for Mrs. Pye. That same rule applied during winter whenever it snowed. If we shoveled snow from our own sidewalk, then we did the same for Mrs. Winston and Mrs. Pye. We were to never charge either of them for the work we did, but if money was offered, Aunt Luebirda said it would be OK to accept it. I recall that Mrs. Winston was pretty good about paying for the work we did. Mrs. Pye wasn't quite as generous.

Though she left school after sixth grade, Aunt Luebirda never lost her desire to learn. She worked diligently to improve her reading and writing skills. She would spend hours late at night reading the newspaper, often highlighting certain points in articles to later share with Arnie and me. Aunt Luebirda believed in correcting us when we did something wrong, which happened perhaps more times than I can remember. But she didn't always use spankings as a means of punishment. Often, she would lecture us for as much as 45 minutes instead. I often wished she had opted to just spank us and be done with it. As I grew older, however, I came to realize that Aunt Luebirda was more than lecturing us. She was giving us "teaching moments." It was her way of preparing us for what lay ahead as we grew into adulthood.

That, I believe, was because Aunt Luebirda saw something in me that I wouldn't see for a long, long time.

I remember her telling me once that I would make my mark in the world, but that there would be challenging times along the way. She said many of the things I would accomplish would not necessarily benefit me, but that they would benefit my children and grandchildren. She called me a trailblazer, and said that at some point I would find myself as the only black person, or one of a few blacks, in the group.

People were watching me, she said, and some were looking for the good in me while others were focusing on my faults. If I did what was right, then I would not have to worry about what others thought of me. She encouraged me to always do my best and to not settle for just doing good or just enough. She said that I represented my family, my neighborhood and my race, and any failure on my part would be a reflection on everything I represented.

Looking back, that was quite a challenge to put on the head of a 9-year-old. But Aunt Luebirda always meant well in what she said to Arnie and me, and how she encouraged us. Besides, she was a woman of faith who loved God and prayed all the time. I would sometimes hear her talking in the middle of the night and wonder who she was talking to. Then, I would realize she was praying to God. Sometimes, her praying would become loud and I could hear her calling out Arnie's and my names.

Aunt Luebirda would pray every night, without fail. Except on Mondays, when professional wrestling came on the TV at 10:30. She loved to watch wrestling, and was a huge fan of a wrestler named Verne Gagne. She would yell and scream just as loud during the wrestling matches as she did when she was praying for Arnie and me. But when wrestling was over, she never failed to take time out to pray to God.

As the school year progressed things got better between my schoolmates and me. I believe the fact that I was able to hold my own during the "crowing" fights, and that I excelled in the classroom, helped me to earn their respect and become accepted.

I liked my fourth-grade teacher, Mrs. Goode. She was very kind and took the time to help me to become acclimated to my new school. Mrs. Goode lived a few blocks down from us, and I later learned she and her husband owned a barbecue restaurant called Skeet's. I remembered seeing it the day we arrived in Omaha, during the taxi ride from the bus station to Aunt Luebirda's house. Even after I moved on to the fifth grade,

Mrs. Goode continued to encourage me.

During the spring of my fourth-grade year, Aunt Luebirda signed me up for the Cub Scouts and Arnie joined the Boy Scouts. The next year, I joined the Boy Scouts. The summer months following my fourth grade year went by quickly. I spent most of the time with the neighborhood kids, playing baseball, basketball and football. By the end of the summer, I was excited, ready to return to Howard Kennedy to begin fifth grade.

Classrooms for fifth graders were on the second floor, which was exciting because it mean Arnie and I would have our classes on the same floor. As it turned out, my fifth-grade teacher would be my favorite. Her name was Mrs. Johnson. She would begin every school day with prayer, something that reminded me a lot of Aunt Luebirda.

Under her tutelage I excelled in all subjects, especially math. On occasion, Mrs. Johnson would have a math contest among the students, the object of which was to see who could solve the problem the fastest. Each participant would stand at the chalkboard and write down the math problem. We would then turn and face Mrs. Johnson, and on her signal turn back to the board and begin solving the math problem. The first student to get the correct answer was declared the winner.

In most cases, I was the winner.

One time, Mrs. Johnson and the sixth-grade teacher decided to have the winners from fifth and sixth grades compete. Surprisingly, Arnie had won the sixth-grade competition. With all the fifth- and sixth-graders present to witness the competition, we squared off to solve not one, but three math problems. I won by solving the first problem the fastest, and Arnie won the second. When it came time for the third problem to be solved, I was nervous. I'm sure Arnie was, too. In the end, the third contest ended in a tie.

The summer of 1955 turned out to very eventful for me. But it would also serve to be a turning point in my life.

Just after the school year ended in June of that year, our social worker, Mrs. Hampton, who had been assigned to us shortly after we arrived in Nebraska, asked Arnie and me if we would like to be adopted by our aunt and uncle. At that point, our father was still our legal guardian. Since we had arrived in Nebraska, Mrs. Hampton had made regular visits to our home to check on us and the relationship we had with Aunt Luebirda and Uncle Cornelius. Of course, we had no complaints about our living arrangements. In fact, we pretty much looked at our aunt and uncle as our parents anyway. So, we agreed to the adoption.

On the day the adoption was to become final, Arnie and I arrived with our aunt and uncle at the courthouse in downtown Omaha. As we climbed the stairs inside the courthouse building, I glanced outside at the Greyhound bus station across the street—the station we had arrived at when we first came to Omaha two years earlier. I thought about how much my life had changed in that short amount of time.

And now, it was about to change even more.

The adoption process could have been stopped had my birth father showed up to contest the proceedings. But he didn't, and in short order the judge granted the petition. After making his ruling, the judge gave Arnie and me the option of choosing what our new names would be.

Arnie chose to be called Cornelius Arnold Jr., after our uncle.

I had not thought about a total name change, but after my brother stated his desire to have a new name, I felt I should do the same. The first name that came to mind was the name of the most popular boy in the class. His name was Harry.

On that day in in 1955, I, Lonnie Tatum Jr., became Harry Arnold.

Flight Log:
This Side of the Tracks

As we prepare to pass over our next checkpoint, I think about contingencies if a major problem were to occur. I remember such occasions: one as I was flying from Denver to Houston and the oil pressure in one of the engines began to decrease. After shutting down the engine, I diverted the plane to Amarillo. I later received a letter from the chief pilot thanking me for saving the company $3 million.

The second incident, which also involved an engine problem, occurred just after taking off from Orange County, California, headed to Denver. Normally, an aircraft would try to return to the airport of departure if a problem occurred just after takeoff. But because Orange County has a short runway, a single engine landing on that runway was out of the question. Los Angeles International Airport was only about 15 minutes away, but weather problems were preventing several aircraft from landing there. My only other option was to try and touch down in San Francisco. Not wanting to attempt flying around the San Gabreal Mountain range with a full load of passengers and only one operating engine, I opted to approach Los Angeles International.

Thankfully, the plane landed safely.

The controller gave me directions to line up for an extended final approach at the Los Angeles airport. The winds were gusty during the approach and landing, but I was able to fly the aircraft to a safe landing. To this day, I am still waiting for my share of the money for saving the engine, and also for a letter from the chief pilot. Of course, I'm just joking!

Finding diversion airports is not as easy on international flights as it is with domestic flights. I experienced that once when I had to divert a flight while going from Newark to Madrid, Spain. We diverted to Lisbon, Portugal, after a passenger started having breathing problems. We were an hour and a half late arriving in Madrid but thankfully, after being turned over to a medical team, the passenger was taken to a medical facility for treatment. I later found out he was doing well.

Today there will be no diversions, no distractions. Only, I did receive a radio call from the pilot of a Delta flight that was in the same airspace as we were. He had heard that I was flying my retirement flight and wanted to wish me well. He also suggested I leave some fish for those pilots who would be following me in retirement. It was a very kind gesture!

Chapter 4

Wagon Boys

Riding home from the courthouse, I reflected on what had just happened. For sure, I would have to get accustomed to my new name. I thought about our new "parents," who Arnie and I would now call "Mom" and "Dad." And I thought about my real mom. I had pretty much been on a rollercoaster since her death, feeling abandoned and no longer with any identity. But the adoption proceedings had taken care of that. Lonnie Tatum Jr. had been replaced by Harry Arnold. And for the first time in my young life, my parents and I shared the same last name!

Bring On the Wagons!

Soon after our adoption, Arnie and I got jobs delivering newspapers for the Omaha World Herald—seven days a week! Every afternoon we would pick up our papers at a designated spot—where several other carriers came to get their papers—and prepare them for delivery. We carried the newspapers in a big sack draped over our shoulders. Most of the time the papers were light and easy to carry. But they were extra heavy on Thursdays, Fridays and especially on Sundays because that was when the area stores advertised their sales and included coupons in the newspaper. They called them "inserts."

Because the newspapers tended to get heavy, our parents decided to buy Arnie and me each a Radio Flyer wagon to help transport our newspapers. Once we started making money, the understanding was that we would pay them back.

Our wagons became a big part of our lives—in more than one way!

When we weren't using our wagons to deliver newspapers, we would ride them up and down the sidewalks on the street where we lived. We became proficient at riding our wagons with our right leg bent at the knee inside the wagon bed, and peddling with the left leg outside the wagon. In this position we would use our right hand on the wagon handle to steer the wagon and our left hand on the front left side of the wagon for balance. We even had races with our neighborhood friends who had bicycles. Before long, Arnie and I had been given the nickname of "The Wagon Boys."

Each day after school, Arnie and I would leave home around 3:00 to deliver papers. It took us about 15 minutes to walk to the pick-up point where the delivery truck dropped off the newspapers, mainly because we were pulling our wagons. The Omaha World Herald delivery truck usually dropped off the newspapers around 3:30, then we would load up our papers, and head out to deliver them. Arnie and I divided the papers according to the number of houses we each had to deliver to. Mine were on Spencer Street, and those he delivered to were on Wirt Street. We both usually delivered to a few houses on 30th Street.

Throwing papers was fun. That's what it was called back then, because we would literally roll each newspaper, put a rubber band around it, and throw it in the direction of each house. The object was to get the paper to land on the front porch. That way, the customer could just walk outside, pick up the paper, and go back inside. That wasn't always the case, though. Lots of times our aim was off and the newspapers landed in the front yards. A few times our throw was too high and a paper might end up on a rooftop. And if our aim was really off, we might break a window.

Probably the only time throwing papers wasn't fun was when we encountered dogs that chased and threatened to bite us. I got bitten twice—by the same dog. One of those times, the dog's owner had told me that if his dog ever charged at me, then

I should just stand still and not try to run. Eventually, he said, the dog would lose interest and walk away. That might have been good advice, but unfortunately the dog never got that memo. The one time he did charge me, and I stood still and didn't run, he bit me anyway.

Delivering newspapers was pretty routine during the weekdays and on Saturdays. Sundays were different, though, because we had to get up early, usually around 4 a.m., so people would have their papers by 7 a.m. One good thing about being a paperboy is that it gave me my first real taste of what it was like to be in business. That's because in addition to delivering the newspapers, we had to collect the payments each week from our customers. I didn't know what it meant then, but for all practical purposes, we were contractors who bought the newspapers from the Omaha World Herald, sold subscriptions to customers, and then paid Omaha World each week after collecting from the customers.

The problem was getting paid.

For the most part, people paid for the newspaper subscriptions on time. But occasionally there were customers who didn't pay on time and would ask us to come back and collect later. If we had a good collection week, we could pay our bill with the Omaha World Herald and have maybe $5 to $10 left for ourselves. Sometimes, because of those customers who didn't pay, we wouldn't make any money at all.

More Heart-Breaking News!

With the adoption process now complete, and Arnie and I settled in at school, things were finally looking up. Three years had passed since our mother's death, and we had begun to look to a fulfilling future. In addition, I had also begun to feel that I was getting close to fulfilling the promise I had made to my real mother that I would stay close to Arnie. I also felt I would be able to keep the promise I made to my new adoptive parents.

Then, in July 1955, there was another shake-up. We received word that Grandma Della had suddenly taken ill while on vacation in Beaumont, Texas. Beaumont had been her first stop on an extended trip she was making to visit family in California, Nebraska, Louisiana and Missouri. When she got the news, mom immediately headed to Beaumont. Unfortunately, Grandma Della passed away just after she arrived.

It wasn't clear from the beginning what caused Grandma Della's sickness. Sometime later, though, we learned that foul play was involved. Apparently, Grandma Della was carrying a lot of money while traveling. Someone found out about the money and supposedly put poison in the drinking water Grandma Della used to take her blood pressure medicine.

That person was eventually charged, convicted and sent to prison.

When my mother returned home from Grandma Della's funeral, Bobby, our half-brother, came with her. Bobby had been living in Standard with Grandma Della. It was the first time the three of us, Arnie, Bobby and I, lived together under the same roof as a family.

When the new school year started in the fall of 1955, my two brothers and I were all attending the same school for the first time since the school year ended in 1953—when we all lived in Olla. Arnie and Bobby were in the same grade, and I was a year behind them.

Now that Bobby was living with us, things changed a bit. For one, it started costing our parents more to care for us because there was another mouth to feed. To help offset that, our mom took on work outside the home two days a week as a housekeeper for a white family. Since they didn't live close by, our mom had to take the bus to work and back each day. On the two days she went to work, my brothers and I would sit on the porch steps of our house and wait for her to return home. When we saw her step off the bus, we would run to greet her. Just like our real mother used to do, Luebirda would have a piece of candy or a snack for us when we came to meet her.

Sixth grade brought several new things to my life. For one,

I found myself interested in music—primarily because of my music teacher. Mrs. Myers took a special interest in me and even said she thought I would someday become a good singer. She also thought Arnie was an excellent student, and told me that she saw the same qualities in me. I took that as a compliment, as I had a lot of respect for my brother and didn't mind at all following in his footsteps. Arnie had been like a father figure to me after the death of our mother, even though he was only two years older. Arnie was almost like a hero to me. He was a hardworking and conscientious student. Through his diligent efforts, Arnie had overcome his stuttering problem. I decided to use my brother's success in school as a motivation for me to succeed also.

I took over Arnie's paper route after he was given a route closer to where we lived. And Bobby even got his own route.

The three of us also joined a youth basketball league, sponsored by the Hope Lutheran Church. We mainly attended church during basketball season so we would be eligible to play on the church basketball team. We teamed up with the pastor's two sons, who were pretty good players, and ended up winning about half our games. While I enjoyed playing church league basketball, I looked forward to seventh grade where I would be eligible to play basketball. Howard Kennedy only had organized team sports for the seventh- and eighth-grade boys.

But church played a more important role in our lives back then than just a means for us to play basketball. My parents were members of St. John AME Church, and they saw to it that my brothers and I were always in church on Sunday. In fact, we had to get up early on Sunday mornings to deliver our newspapers so we would be in Sunday school on time. Most often, we would come home from running our paper routes, take a short nap, and then make the 20-minute walk with our parents to church.

I remember the Sunday morning Arnie, Bobby and I joined the church. It was during a special service, and we were told our names would become part of the church's permanent records. For some reason, that just sounded very special to us. We also participated in most all the youth activities at the church.

Sometimes, we got to go to the movies after church on Sundays. The two movie theaters in the black community only showed second-run movies, so our preference was to go downtown to either the Omaha or Orpheum theaters, which always showed the newest movies. Sometimes, we got a bonus because those theaters would show a first-run movie, and then add a second feature at no extra charge.

I guess somebody forgot to tell the folks in Omaha about Jim Crow, because we got to sit where we wanted in the theater—including the balcony—which we often did. I guess old habits are hard to break.

Another Moment of Tragedy

In the spring of my sixth grade year, my uncle Frank was diagnosed with cancer. He died a short time after that. The loss of her brother took a serious toll on my mom. Within three years, she had lost her youngest sister, her mother and now her only brother. Even though Uncle Frank was her half brother, she was still very close to him. When he first moved to Omaha in the late 1930s, Uncle Frank had lived in my mother's home for a short time.

My mom was a strong woman, though. It was clear to me that the family, mostly her siblings, looked to her as the one to take charge of when certain situations arose—especially when there was a death in the family. In times like that, my mom simply put aside her personal grief and did what was needed to ensure things were taken care of. I loved that about her!

During the summer of 1956, I joined a Little League baseball team. I think I became interested in baseball because of the time I spent on Saturday afternoons with my dad, watching baseball on TV. Our favorite team was the Brooklyn Dodgers—mainly because they were the first major league team to have a black player—Jackie Robinson.

Watching baseball games was probably the most quality time I ever spent with Dad. Sometimes on Saturday mornings, I would come into the kitchen for breakfast and he would be sitting at the table reading his Bible. He would stop reading and ask me how to pronounce a certain word. I would pronounce the word, and then give him a brief explanation of what the word meant.

I had been fortunate to have excellent teachers since coming to Howard Kennedy, and my seventh grade-teacher, Mrs. Foreman, was no exception. Just like my other teachers, Mrs. Foreman, who, by the way, was white, was a great motivator. She wanted her students to be successful, so she always pressed them to do their best. She would often query me about my desires and plans for the future. At that young age, I was pretty much like most every other child who thought they wanted to be a doctor, fireman or even a school teacher. Although I never gave it much thought, I did have a feeling I would somehow be involved in education.

Seventh grade was also an introduction to my somewhat short-lived career as a singer. Arnie and I started a singing group called "The Wonders" with two of our classmates, Larry and Lloyd. Arnie wrote the lyrics for our songs, and we would practice in our home, with our parents' permission of course. None of us played instruments, but we did have bunch of 33 and 45 rpm records that we practiced by, using a hand crank Motorola record player. Later in the school year, we got to perform at a youth variety show.

One highlight of the term was when Howard Kennedy's eighth-grade flag football team won the North Omaha championship and went on to defeat the South Omaha champions for the city championship. The star player for Howard Kennedy was a young black kid named Gale Sayers, who would go on to become a star player with the National Football League's Chicago Bears and eventually be inducted into the NFL Hall of Fame.

Arnie and I remained very active in the Boys Scouts during those years as well. While I worked to become a Life Scout, Arnie was working toward becoming an Eagle Scout. He reached that goal shortly after the school year ended, and right after that he and two other students had been become recipients of the Howard Kennedy Rotary Honor Society award. I was so proud of

Arnie, who was such a role model for me in so many ways. When school started in the fall of 1957, our parents decided that Arnie and I would attend Central High School, whose racial makeup was 75 percent white, 20 percent Jewish and 5 percent black. I still had one year to go before entering high school, but Arnie would start that year.

Central had high academic standards, and had recently been ranked No. 38 in the nation for academic achievement. The school's curriculum was designed primarily to prepare students for college. The alternative to Central was a local technical high school. Though the technical school did prepare students for college, its main focus was to help them prepare for technical careers following graduation from high school. Bobby had already decided he wanted to attend technical school, but as for Arnie and me, our mother had made it clear that, even though she didn't know where the finances would come from, we would go to college. She loved and trusted God, and she just believed that, somehow, He would make a way for us to go to school.

Eighth grade was a busy year, with me being involved in a number of activities, including being captain of the Safety Patrol Squad, playing on the school's basketball team, and receiving the Rotary Club Award. Yes, I guess you could say I was following in my brother's footsteps. My parents surprised me by buying me a new charcoal gray suit to wear to the Rotary Club luncheon and my graduation ceremony. I remember it well, because it was the first time I'd ever had a brand new suit—and not one that was handed down from someone else. After moving to Omaha, many of our clothes had been given to us by the family our mother worked for as a housekeeper.

In the fall of 1958, I enrolled at Central High School. Once again, Arnie and I were together in the same school. I felt like I was riding the crest of an ocean wave. What could go wrong?

Little did I know, but I was about to receive an answer to that question.

✈ Flight Log: Mid-Atlantic

Just prior to reaching the midpoint of our flight across the Atlantic, we are notified that our meal is ready. For a brief moment, I reflect on what mealtime was like when I first began flying with Continental years ago, and was a second officer (flight engineer) to the captain (pilot) and first officer (co-pilot).

The three meals available to us then were usually one steak dinner and two chicken dinners. Since the captain and the first officer would be eating different meals, it was always likely the second officer (me) would end up eating chicken. On occasion, the lead flight attendant would have an extra first-class meal and would make it available to one of us.

Over the years, and with Americans becoming more health conscious, crew meals aboard aircraft have changed. Today, the choice is either steak OR chicken. You guessed it, I still chose steak. After all, it IS my last meal on the flight deck!

Following our meal, we engage in more checkpoint details, including considering where I would divert the aircraft were some emergency to arise. The closet airport was Reykjavik, Iceland, which was only about one and one-half hours flying time away. I had never flown into Reykjavik, but I had viewed pictorials of the airport and was familiar with the layout of the airport. A pilot once told me that there was a pretty woman behind every tree in Iceland. The problem with that, though, was that there aren't many trees in Iceland.

So much for that!

As we depart Shanwick airspace and enter Gander airspace, the aircraft automatically sends both control centers notification of our location. I recalled the time years back when such reports had to be made verbally over High Frequency (HF) radio, which sometimes created problems because the radio frequencies were very sensitive to weather changes—especially during a thunderstorm. Technology changed that.

With all the checkpoint responsibilities completed, my thoughts return, once again, to my retirement. I think about Christine, and all the hard work she has done with the planning of the entire weekend affair. But that's the kind of person she is. When she puts her mind to do something, she gets it done—no questions asked!

I also think about my good friends, Nancy and Othe, who are part of my traveling party. Their daughter had remained behind in Newark instead of coming along on the retirement flight, to make final arrangements for the party. She, too, had put in a lot of work in planning for the party.

I think how blessed I am to have a wife like Christine, and such good friends as Nancy and Othe in my life. Then my thoughts turn to my brother. I wonder if he is still working on his speech for tonight.

Part 2

Chapter 5

Separation

One morning as I was headed into my English class, Arnie came up and said he wouldn't be walking home with me after school. I knew he had been dealing with some kind of flu bug, so I wasn't overly concerned. When I got home that afternoon, I learned that a stomach flu wasn't the reason Arnie had left school early that day. Instead, I was told that my parents had decided to send Arnie to live in a boys home until he graduated from school.

Talk about shock and surprise!

I knew there had been a growing differences of opinions between Arnie and our parents. I had seen evidence of a gap between them widening little by little with each passing day. I didn't know the exact nature of the conflict, nor did I ever ask. I suppose I thought if I ignored the situation, it would eventually go away. As I grew older, however, I learned that the reasons for conflict between two people are sometimes not easily defined. I also learned that the solutions to these conflicts can also be somewhat blurred.

Once the shock of what I had just heard wore off, I became angry—both with my parents and my brother. It was the kind of anger, I later learned, that a child might experience when his or her parents get divorced. There are all kinds of questions like: "Why couldn't they work out their differences?" Or, "Didn't they think about me when they made that decision? Or, "Did I, in some way, cause the breakup?"

As Arnie was packing his bags to leave, there was an eerie

silence in the house. My thoughts were running wild.

Do I insist on going to the boys home with Arnie, or do I stay with our parents?

Arnie must have been reading my mind, because just before leaving he told me to stay with our parents. He said his disagreements with them were his concern and not mine, and that our parents needed me now more than ever. He promised that he would continue working to fulfill the pledge we both had made to our parents when we were adopted, and assured me that everything would be fine.

Bobby and I continued to share the same bedroom. Our parents chose to leave Arnie's room just as it was until he returned home after graduation. Arnie's being away, for me, was subtle, but significant. For the first time in my life, I would not be seeing my brother every day. And that was to be the case for the foreseeable future. The quiet assurance that came with my knowing that my brother was by my side to back me up, especially in a fist fight, was not there any longer. I knew that the time would come when we would separate, especially when Arnie went off to college, but I didn't expect it to happen so soon.

As best I could, in Arnie's absence I went about my daily routine. Deep down inside, though, there was a huge void. Something was missing in my life. A short time after Arnie left home, my parents shared with me about the family finances. One significant thing was that my father would be retiring from his job as a meat cutter with the Swift Meat Packing Company in 1962, the same year I would be graduating from high school. His pension would be considerably less than the paycheck he was used to bringing home, which mean an obvious decrease in the family's monthly income. What became apparent to me right away about the family finances was that the second mortgage and the increase in food costs had put a strain on the family finances. Based on what I was hearing, it was clear to me that my parents would be hard-pressed financially when it came time for me to go to college. But that wasn't a major concern for me. My focus was to do whatever I could to help them financially.

I set up a budget for the family's weekly income which, in most cases, my parents agreed with. Whenever I made a suggestion they didn't agree with regarding the finances, my mother would always explain their reasoning or say she would pray and seek God before making a decision.

It's interesting how that one simple gesture began to bring my mother and me closer together. Over time, we talked a lot about a number of things, including civil rights issues. We discussed things like the Brown vs. Board of Education Supreme Court case, and we talked about the death of Emmitt Teal, a 14-year-old black kid from Chicago who was killed in August 1955 while visiting relatives in Mississippi. According to reports, Teal was beaten and then lynched for allegedly making a pass at a white woman. Teal was reportedly beaten so badly that his face was unrecognizable. During his funeral, Teal's mother insisted that his casket be opened so the public could see the beating her son endured.

We also talked a lot about Dr. Martin Luther King Jr. and his nonviolent methods for bringing about change among the races in our country. It was very apparent to me that my mother had much respect for Dr. King, and high hopes for what he would accomplish because his supporters consisted of both blacks and whites.

Freshman Year at Central High

After establishing a firm academic foundation my freshman year at Central, I tried out for the freshman basketball team. Not only did I make the team, but I made the starting lineup for the first game. Freshman basketball games were played on Saturday mornings. That particular season, the freshman team only lost two games. But that didn't make us anything special, because not many people paid much attention to the freshman team. Usually only a handful of parents even came out on Saturday mornings to watch the team play. When the season ended, I was proud to look back and say I was able to juggle basketball and a paper route, and still maintain a high grade-point average in school.

During the summer, I enrolled in a sophomore biology course at the technical high school. I had heard from other students that the course was very intense and would require a lot of homework during the school year. Since I wanted to play junior varsity basketball during the upcoming season, I decided that by taking the biology course during the summer, I would have one less challenging course to deal with during the regular school year. I also took clarinet lessons that summer, but after a while I got a little slack and my parents cancelled my lessons.

School without Arnie was not much fun. I missed him a lot.

During my sophomore year, I met Arlene. Though neither of us ever let on that we had feelings for the other, there may have been a flicker of a flame there somewhere. But nothing ever came of it. I met Arlene while working as a hall monitor—a position I assumed after voluntarily giving up my daily study hall. I was assigned the north hallway, and that's where I saw Arlene for the first time.

Friendly and outgoing, Arlene was a joy to talk with and to be around. I soon discovered that she was just as beautiful on the inside as she was on the outside. Since neither she nor I were looking for a romantic relationship, there was no pressure in just being friends. With each passing day Arlene made a point to stop by the north hallway while I was on duty. Since we did not share any classes, this was the only time for us to talk during the school day. During our conversations I mentioned that I would be trying out for the junior varsity basketball team in the fall. Arlene said that she would be cheering for me because she intended to try out for the school's pep squad.

When time came to try out for varsity basketball, I was one of about 50 players vying for 13 spots. Unfortunately, I didn't make the cut and ended up on the junior varsity team. Though disappointed, I welcomed the opportunity to play basketball, no matter which team I was on.

Since my parents didn't own a car, I had to ride the city bus to all the home games, which were played at Norris Junior High School. Getting to the games was no problem, but because the last bus leaving Norris each evening always left before the games ended, I had no way to get home. Little did I know that my friendship with Arlene would provide a solution to my transportation problem. Arlene had, in fact, made the pep squad and was driven to the games by her mother. Most of the time, Arlene's mother was more than happy to give me a ride home after my games.

The highlight of the season for me that year came during one of our home games. The score was tied with only 10 seconds remaining on the clock. I received the inbound pass, dribbled the entire length of the court, and scored the winning basket just before the buzzer sounded. Excited and overjoyed, my teammates celebrated by throwing me into the school's swimming pool.

Near the end of the school year, I got the chance to visit with Arnie at the boys home. Not surprisingly, he was doing well and had continued to excel in sports—specifically football, basketball, and track and field. In fact, Arnie was a member of the mile relay team that won the Nebraska State championship. The Omaha World Herald printed a very nice article about the team. I was very proud of Arnie and his accomplishments.

During the summer, I took a job as a door-to-door salesman for Fuller Brush Company. My primary sales territory was the eastern part of North Omaha, in what were racially mixed but predominately white neighborhoods. There were good sales days, and then I had some really bad days. Some of my potential customers, for instance, would invite me into their homes to display my products while other individuals would answer the door and say no even before I got a chance to give my sales pitch. Some simply pretended to not be home, even though I could hear the sounds of a radio or TV coming from inside. When I wasn't peddling Fuller Brush products, I did odd jobs for Mrs. Pye, Mrs. Winston and some of the other neighbors.

It was during this summer that I began to have talks with my mother about religion. Even though I was baptized as a boy I really didn't feel a closeness to God. This could have been due to the fact that I was still young. Or it could have been because I was still trying to understand a God who allowed my mother to die when I was only 6 years old. I sometimes thought, *If this is an attribute of a loving God, then I would hate to see what He does when He's angry.*

All that changed, though, through a relationship my mother had with my caseworker, Mrs. Hampton.

Although both my parents were members of St. John AME Church, my mother attended church only twice a month while my father went on a more regular basis. Bobby and I went because we had no other choice.

Over time, my mother had established a friendship relationship with Mrs. Hampton beyond the fact that she had been Arnie's and my caseworker when we first moved to Omaha in 1953. Mrs. Hampton was a Seventh Day Adventist, a church denomination that recognizes Saturday as the Sabbath instead of Sunday. On one occasion, Mrs. Hampton had invited my mother to visit her church. Before long, my mother was going on a regular basis.

I remember the first time I went with her.

Though I knew nothing about Seventh Day Adventists, I was surprisingly impressed with their service. I especially enjoyed the preaching and the music. The pastor's wife, who was the choir director, played piano. I remember wondering why it was that in most churches the pastor's wife also played piano. Was having a wife who played piano some kind of prerequisite to becoming a pastor?

I liked the church enough that I wanted to become a member. But that meant making several adjustments in my young life—including the fact that I could not work on Saturdays. The Seventh Day Adventists believed in the sacredness of the Sabbath, which was observed from sundown on Friday until sundown on Saturday. I continued to attend the church, and just before my junior year started, my mother and I became members of Sharon Seventh Day Adventist Church. Later that year my father and Bobby joined as well.

Joining Sharon SDA Church helped me in a number of ways, including the fact that I began to view God in a different way. I stopped blaming Him for my mother's death. I came to realize that, even though God allows certain things to happen, He doesn't always cause them to happen. When someone is facing challenging times in their life, God is always there to comfort them. I began to see that the death of my mother was a tragedy, and that only God could help me erase the pain that was in my heart.

I didn't know it then, but I would soon learn that my newfound faith would have one serious drawback.

My junior year at Central was to serve as my year of transition as I prepared for college. In addition to focusing on academics, I was also intent on completing my last two years as a member of the varsity basketball team. I was a bit devastated when I learned that my religion forbade me from playing sports on Friday evenings, the time when most of Central's basketball games were played. The question loomed largely over my head: Do I play basketball the final two years, or do I honor my commitment to my faith and my beliefs? I'd love to say it was an easy decision to make, but it wasn't. Realizing that my days of playing basketball would someday fade away, but my faith in God would remain with me for the remainder of my life, I made the wise choice and decided to step away from basketball.

A Second Hallway Experience

Standing in the hallway one day, I happened to look up just in time to see a young girl trip and fall while coming down the stairs. I rushed over to gather her books, which were scattered from the fall. Over the next few weeks, we became closer and eventually started dating.

Though I had strong feelings for this girl, I was careful to not allow anything to interfere with my plans for the future. During the summer between my junior and senior years, I worked as a busboy at a restaurant. Then, when school started in the fall, I began to set my sights on college. My goal for the year was to finish strong and hope for an academic scholarship at the end of the school year. Arnie, who had continually done well academically, was already college-bound with plans of studying medicine.

Deciding on which college to attend was only part of the dilemma I was facing. The biggest issue was finances because of my father's impending retirement after 42 years at the meat-packing plant. His retirement income would only be a portion of what he was earning, so the likelihood of him being able to help with college tuition and expenses was very slim.

The logical decision would have been to attend Omaha University, which was local. That's where many of the students who graduated from Central went, for at least two reasons—it was local, and it didn't cost much. Wichita State University in Kansas, caught my attention, but attending that school would be a financial stretch because of the high tuition. The University of Nebraska in Lincoln was a good compromise because it was only about 60 miles from Omaha, which meant I would be able to come home on weekends. Eventually, I settled on the University of Nebraska. Though tuition was $1200 a year, it included books, plus room and board. Once I was accepted to the University of Nebraska, I was awarded two $300 scholarships, which left me owing only $600 per year. I had some money saved from working during the summer, but not enough to pay the difference. So, I found work through an employment agency and was able to make enough money to pay the rest.

The first job, working at the meat-packing plant, was only a two-week assignment. The second job, at an auto-painting shop, lasted much longer and paid enough for me to make up the difference in my tuition. The owner was glad to know I was going to college. I worked alongside several older black men, who were also proud of me for deciding to go to college.

The job paid $35 a week, a lot of money for a young kid growing up in those days. Whenever I got my paycheck, I divided the money according to a financial plan I had worked out for myself. First, I took out 10 percent, or $3.50 for my church tithe. That was something I learned from my mother. Giving God what belongs to Him is important. Then, I designated $3.50 for my weekly spending money, and $8 for my family's household expenses. The year before, my mother had opened a joint savings account for herself and me, where I could deposit money to help pay for my college. I set aside the remaining $20 each week to deposit into that account.

When I arrived on the University of Nebraska campus in the fall of 1962, I was one of only 40 blacks out of a total enrollment of about 12,000 students, and one of only a handful of blacks on academic scholarship. The majority of the black students were on athletic scholarships. Not only that, but only two of the black students were female, which immediately established limitations for any social life the black male students might have hoped for.

To make matters worse, the city of Lincoln had a small black population, and the black males in that black community didn't take too kindly to the black male students from NU dating "their women." Interracial dating was taboo as well, because the university's white males did not want the black male students dating "their women." Needless to say, the black male students found themselves in a tough situation when it came to dating.

Freshman year was what most would consider typical. I registered for 15 credit hours, the norm for students hoping to graduate in four years. And for work-study, which was part of the terms of my scholarship, I was assigned to wash pots and pans in the dining hall of Bessey Hall, the men's dormitory, for 12 to 15 hours each week.

I declared electrical engineering as my major area of study. It would be two years before I would start taking any core courses in my major field of study. Several of my classes were in a large classroom with the instructor using the lecture method of teaching. The students were very knowledgeable which one would expect from college students.

I wish I could say my freshman year was a breeze. Unfortunately, that wasn't the case. And it was all my fault. Early into the first semester, I was invited to play on the Bessey flag football team. Even though my schedule was very tight already, I chose to play because of my love for sports, particularly football and basketball. The team had a successful run, winning the dormitory league championship and then going on to compete in the overall university championship. I even scored three touchdowns in the championship game, which we lost by a score of 25-18. The bad news, though, was that while I was having fun playing flag football, I was also getting behind in my studies. The end result was that I ended up being placed on academic probation that semester. And, had I not cleaned up my act and got my grades back in order, I would have lost my scholarships.

The worst part for me, though, was how my failure affected my mother. She was completely devastated upon learning that I had fallen down. I felt I had let her and everyone else down, and that made me sick to my stomach. I promised I would make things right and that it would never happen again, which seemed to make her feel better. As a start, I stepped away from sports of any kind and put my sole concentration on getting my grades back in order.

Second semester, things were different.

I worked diligently at getting my grades up, and was no longer on academic probation. That's when I bought my first car—a gray, four-door 1950 Ford that cost me a whopping $50. My parents were pleasantly surprised to see my new car, although initially my mother was hesitant to ride with me. But over time, they both became comfortable and readily took short rides with me.

Fraternal Order

November 22, 1963, would be turn out to be a day I would remember for the rest of my life. On the previous evening, the Kappa Alpha Psi pledges had our heads shaved as part of a fraternity initiation exercise. It was the first time my head was completely bald since I was a little boy in Olla. At 12:30 p.m. local time the following day, I was just finishing my midday shift of washing pots and pans in the dining room when it was announced on TV that President John F. Kennedy had been assassinated. As the news spread throughout the dining room and kitchen, a hush suddenly fell over the entire place. As I walked back to my dorm room to prepare for my afternoon American history class, I noticed that the campus seemed to be eerily quiet. When I entered my classroom, most of the students had blank stares on their faces. A few talked in hushed tones. The instructor tried to initiate a discussion about American history, but his efforts were fruitless. After about 15 minutes, he dismissed the class.

The mood around campus over the next few days was very somber. With Thanksgiving just a few days away, it provided the perfect opportunity for us all to get away, and perhaps direct our thoughts elsewhere. Of course, the reality was that being away from school wasn't going to help any of us forget the tragedy that had befallen our nation. That was something that only time could heal.

Just before Christmas break, 17 other pledgees and I crossed over and became full-fledged members of the ETA chapter of Kappa Alpha Psi fraternity. I was subsequently elected as treasurer for the chapter. Near the end of the spring semester, I applied to NU's advanced Air Force Reserve Officers Training Corps (ROTC).

Summer wasn't as much fun as I had hoped—for several reasons—but mostly because of the fact that I couldn't find a job.

The auto-painting company I'd worked for the previous summer had experienced a downturn in business, as was the case with most companies due to Omaha's declining economy, and the owner wasn't able to offer me a job. That created a serious problem because I was counting on the income from that job to help with tuition for the next school year. I sought employment elsewhere, but there was nothing available.

When it looked like I would not be returning to school for my junior year, it quickly became apparent that I needed to be considering other alternatives regarding my future. The fact that I was 18 and not in school was a sure bet that I would become a prime candidate for the draft—something I wasn't particularly interested in at the time. I loved my country, and had no problem serving in the military. But when that time came, I wanted to be the one to make that decision.

By mid-August, I had begun giving serious consideration to possible options to returning to school. One was enlisting in the military. That way I could continue working on my college education and serve my country at the same time. I took the Air Force entrance exam and scored high in the area of electronics. The recruiter said the fact that I had two years of college meant I would receive my first stripe during basic training. It also meant my monthly pay would be a little more than other recruits. After giving the matter much thought, I decided to enlist in the Air Force. I returned the scholarship money I had received from the local National Urban League, and informed NU officials that I would not be using the loan and scholarship funds the coming year.

On September 1, 1964, I boarded a plane to fly to San Antonio, Texas. It was my first time on an airplane and, to be honest, I was nervous about flying. But those fears were quickly calmed, however, as we made stops along the way. Something about those takeoffs and landings fascinated me! At 11:30 that night, we arrived in San Antonio. The next day, at Lackland Air Force Base, I enlisted in the United States Air Force.

Flight Log: The Other Side of the Tracks

We are now approaching the eastern coast of Newfoundland. Following this checkpoint, we head through Kobey and into Gander Domestic Center's airspace. Gander has the capability of displaying our aircraft's exact position in its airspace and has more positive radar control of inbound aircraft. At this point, the first officer and I start our "coast in" checklist, the final computations on our oceanic maps and charts.

Now, we enter the final, third portion of the flight.

Flying over Newfoundland, I'm reminded of an experience a little over four years ago by a fellow Continental pilot. Peter had been flying over the same area on September 11, 2001, when he was told by Gander Center that he would not be allowed to enter the United States airspace. Instead, Peter was instructed to land in Newfoundland.

A thousand thoughts were going through Peter's mind after receiving that message, but his immediate thought, he told me, was to secure the flight deck. Peter was not aware of what had happened in New York City, but knew something was gravely wrong.

After informing the crew and passengers of the flight change, Peter landed in Newfoundland. Afterward, he became "land captain" for his crew and passengers, proceeding to arrange hotel accommodations for everyone—a feat that was not easily accomplished because there were not enough hotel rooms available. Subsequently, a number of the passengers ended up being housed by local residents who had apparently heard about the tragic events that had taken place in New York City and wanted to do whatever they could to help.

By now you've likely figured out this was all in the aftermath of the now historic 9/11 terrorist attack on the United States.

After four days of being grounded in Newfoundland, Peter, his crew and their passengers were cleared to continue on to Newark. Peter said that during those four days, many of the people bonded in such a way that, a year later on the anniversary of 911, some of them reunited in Newfoundland.

In this same moment of reflection, I recall the events that occurred in my own life on that Tuesday in September. At that time I was living in Denver, Colorado, but I was based in Newark, New Jersey. I had been scheduled to begin a two-day Newark-to-London trip on September 12, and had planned to commute to Newark on September 11. While getting dressed on the morning of the eleventh, a friend called and told me to turn on my television. When I did, I saw the first of the Twin Towers in flames.

My mind began racing in all directions. Surely, this was a mistake.

As the events of that day continued to unfold, I would later learn that what I was witnessing was not a mistake. It was an event that would not only have a lasting effect on the airline industry, but also on the entire world. Needless to say, I was not able to commute to Newark that day, but instead remained in Denver until September 13, when I flew to Newark to make a three-day flight to Dusseldorf, Germany, on September 14. When I arrived at the Denver airport, I noticed security was very strict. It would be the same upon arriving in Newark. Little did I realize these security measures would become a way of life for the air traveler.

Prior to departure from Newark, we were told that Continental was closing its Dusseldorf station and that ours would be the last flight for Continental from Newark to Dusseldorf.

The announcement was disappointing, considering I always enjoyed my layovers in Dusseldorf. Once we arrive in Dusseldorf, we are given the option of returning immediately as passengers on what would be the final flight from Dusseldorf to Newark or taking ground transportation from Dusseldorf to Frankfurt, Germany, and returning to Newark the following day on another Continental flight. Despite the fact I enjoyed the layovers, we all chose to return immediately to Newark.

Landing in Dusseldorf, we are instructed by the control tower to proceed to a remote area of the airport rather than taxi to the normal parking gate. The aircraft is escorted by a contingent of armed German soldiers riding in armored vehicles. Departing the aircraft, the passengers and crew are loaded onto buses, then escorted to the terminal's customs and immigrations sections. Inside, security measures are even more stringent than they had been back in the United States. We were later told that, in light of what had happen in the United States, German officials had chosen to take extra precaution against any similar attacks.

After clearing customs, we are escorted back to buses and then back to the aircraft. Once aboard, I brief the outbound crew about the events that had taken place in New York. For most onboard, it is just another flight from Dusseldorf to Newark. However, that is not the case for me. Seated in the passenger's cabin, and now traveling as a passenger rather than the flight's captain, I find more time for reflection. Looking out the window as the plane prepares for takeoff, I notice those same armored vehicles escorted the aircraft to the end of the runway. I surmise that all the German army troops will breathe a sigh of relief after the aircraft take off.

Silently, I wondered: *What is this world coming to?*

Chapter 6

Working for Uncle Sam

Since September 2, 1964, was also Labor Day, I expected to be processed into the Air Force the following day. The Air Force had different thoughts, and on that day I found myself in line and slowly moving from one table to the next as I transitioned from being a civilian to a member of the United States Armed Forces.

When I returned to the barracks, the transition was complete. I was armed with a duffel bag filled with military clothing and my head was shaved. Sgt. Gonzales, my training instructor, was a tough instructor who always said he was tough on us for our own good. Someday, he would always say, we would appreciate how he treated us.

It was under Sgt. Gonzales that I learned how to march. I say that jokingly, but in truth it seemed that everywhere we, as recruits, went we marched instead of walked. Either we were marching to the mess hall, or to class. We marched to physical training, and we marched to the parade grounds—where we practiced even more marching. When we weren't marching, we cleaned the barracks. Cleaning those old barracks was like putting makeup on a pig. On the surface it looked good, but it was still a pig. About the only good part of each day was mail call. My friend, Arlene, had been faithful to write to me at least twice a week. I also received letters from my parents, which I always looked forward to. I could tell from the handwriting that my mother was doing most of the writing.

Not long after arriving at Lackland, my mother forwarded

me a letter that had been sent to my home from the University of Nebraska Department of Air Force ROTC. The letter informed me that I had been accepted into the advanced ROTC program. It was not good news, for at least two reasons. First, the letter had arrived after I enlisted in the military. And second, even with the ROTC scholarship I would still not have enough money to cover my college expenses. In any case, I'd already made my choice and I would not be looking back.

At the end of the first phase of basic training, I received my first stripe as I had been promised by my recruiter. The stripe brought with it a nice bump in pay of an additional $20 a month. One other trainee in my barracks who had some college credits also received his first stripe. The other trainees remained as "slick sleeves." It was also during this time that we received our first off-base pass and a chance to visit the beautiful city of San Antonio. In the coming years, San Antonio would become one of my favorite places.

Near the end of basic training, I was asked to fill out a "dream sheet" indicating where I wanted to be assigned for training in the field of electronics. My first choice was Lowry Air Force Base near Denver. I also chose Chanute Air Force Base near Chicago, Illinois. After receiving my assignment, it became obvious why it was called a "dream sheet." Despite expressing my desires for assignment, I was assigned to Keesler Air Force Base near Biloxi, Mississippi.

We traveled to Keesler AFB by bus, passing through several towns, including Beaumont, Texas. Seeing Beaumont for the first time since Grandma Della died there nearly 10 years earlier, I couldn't help but reflect on my past, which in some ways made me sad. When the bus crossed the state line into Mississippi, I saw shotgun houses similar to the one I grew up in while in Louisiana.

Interestingly, during that time the state of Mississippi was in the national spotlight. A civil rights movement called Freedom Summer had been launched to get blacks in the Southern United States to vote. Thousands of students and civil rights activists, both black and white, had traveled to Southern states to register black voters, but the focal point of the civil rights movement was Mississippi. In June of that year three male members of the activist group, one black, one Jewish and one white, suspiciously disappeared while in Mississippi. Two months later, their remains were discovered. Years later, a Mississippi court determined that the local Ku Klux Klan was involved in the mysterious disappearance and subsequent deaths of the three men. Almost 25 years later, a movie, titled "Mississippi Burning," chronicled the role of an FBI investigation and solving of the case.

My electronics course at Keesler lasted three months. The first half of the training covered basic electronics, and the second half focused on my specialty field of radio relay maintenance. Basically, the training would prepare me to maintain and repair microwave communications equipment at remote transmitter facilities. With the escalation of hostile activities in Southeast Asia at the time, military aircraft flying on bombing missions from bases in South Vietnam to enemy targets in North Vietnam would require communications relay equipment during their missions. There was a need for maintenance personnel to maintain these facilities. Not only was my chosen field interesting, it was challenging. And to make it even more interesting, I was the only black airman out of my class of 20 airmen to be in that class. Eventually, I connected with three other blacks who were training in another field of electronics. On weekends the four of us would frequent nightclubs in the black section of Biloxi. At one point, we even pooled our money and bought a car, a 1955 Mercury, so we wouldn't have to rely on public transportation. Since I was not big on drinking, I was usually the designated driver when the four of us went out. The four of us also agreed that when time came for us to be reassigned, the last one to remain at Keeler would become sole owner of the car.

One night as we were returning to the base, a car with four occupants pulled up alongside us. The four occupants inside each wore a white hood. Thinking my friends had been drinking too much to win in a fight, especially with the KKK, I decided to try and outrun the other car, and sped back to Keesler. Fortunately, the occupants of the other car broke off the chase and there was no confrontation.

Overseas-Bound

Near the end of my electronics training I was notified we were being assigned to Clark AFB in the Philippines upon graduation from technical school. Because I was the last of the four of us to leave Keesler, I got to keep the car. Since I couldn't take the car to the Philippines, and didn't want to take it back to Omaha before being deployed, I chose to give the car to another airman who was just beginning the electronics program at Keesler.

In March 1965, I traveled by train from Biloxi to Travis AFB near San Francisco, California. On the way, I stopped off in Omaha to spend a few days with my parents before beginning my overseas tour of duty, which I was told could last as long as three years. Upon graduation from technical school, I was promoted to the rank of airman second class, which saw my monthly salary increase from $60 to $99. Knowing I would have no need for the extra money while overseas, I decided to give my parents $60 each month.

The flight to the Philippines was an interesting one, to say the least. The military aircraft was outfitted with combat passenger seats along the sides of the interior rather than regular airline passenger seats. There were about 100 other military personnel and some military equipment onboard the aircraft. After sitting on those combat seats for a couple of hours, they began to feel more than uncomfortable. I suppose that's why they were called combat seats. After about eight hours in the air, we landed on Wake Island to refuel. Wake Island is not very large. The runway is about the biggest thing on the island. About seven hours later, we arrived at Clark AFB in the Philippines.

Located on about 18,000 acres, Clark was the major staging point for personnel and equipment going to and from military bases in Southeast Asia. The amount of air traffic at the base rivalled that of any stateside major airport. All types of military and contract civilian aircraft landed and departed from the base at all hours of the day and night. Clark was the last stop for troops headed for South Vietnam or Thailand, and the first stop for troops returning from those countries.

Over the next couple of days, I endured the rigorous task of processing before finally receiving my assignment to the 608th Radio Relay Squadron of the 5th Tactical Control Group. Surprisingly, a number of other recruits in my area of specialty were also assigned to the same group. At one point, some of us were used to supplement the Clark's security police by serving as guards. We worked six-hour shifts in the middle of the night, guarding the outer perimeter of the on-base housing area where military personnel and their families lived. We were armed with M16 rifles and two loaded clips of ammunition shells.

Among our other assignments was that of litter bearers. Litter bearers were assigned to unload wounded military troops from Air Force cargo planes and onto awaiting ambulances. We also rode in the ambulances to assist in unloading the wounded once they reached the hospital. Clark had one of the largest military medical facilities in the South Pacific.

The chances of ever handling someone you know who was injured in battle are pretty slim, unless, of course, they had been assigned to your group. But on one occasion, a friend told me that while working as a litter bearer the night before, he had transported someone to Clark hospital who was from my hometown in Omaha. Though I didn't know him, I visited the young soldier who was only 19 years old, while he was in the hospital. He had been injured in a mine accident and had to have a portion of his left leg amputated. Soon after that, he was sent back to the United States.

Though I hadn't been in the military long enough to see actual combat, I was getting a pretty good taste of what it was like just working those various assignments. Being in the military didn't take away my drive and passion for learning. When I was not on duty, I busied myself with taking Air Force sponsored college courses to complete my college education. During my initial visit to the base education office, I met Captain Frank Mayberry, the base education officer. Captain Mayberry was a 1962 graduate of the United States Air Force Academy. After reviewing my educational background and discovering I had spent a brief time as an airman in the Air Force, Captain Mayberry asked if I had considered applying to the academy. He explained that the Air Force reserved a few slots for enlisted airmen who passed the same educational and physical tests as those applicants who had received congressional appointments. Obviously, the thought of being able to complete my college education and get my degree was appealing. But I wasn't too keen on the idea of having to start all over as a freshman and spending another four years in the books. Besides, I had almost completed the first year of my four-year enlistment as an airman, and I would get my discharge from the Air Force in September 1968. If I was successful in applying to the academy, my class starting date would be in June 1966, and I would graduate in June 1970.

Another fact to consider was my age. Even though I had graduated from Central High School at the age of 16, I would still be a couple of years older than the other incoming cadets in my class. Still I was glad to see that Captain Mayberry was taking a personal interest in me. He even offered to help me prepare for the academic and physical exams.

I also got the chance to dabble some in sports when, in the fall of 1965, I joined our group's tackle football team, playing the safety position. The games were a big part of the weekends for the airmen and their families. The 5,000-seat stadium was usually filled to capacity. When we played a team from Guam for the Pacific Championship, a game that ended in a 26-26 tie, the stadium held an overflow crowd of between 7,000 and 8,000.

In February 1966, I got word that I had been accepted into the Air Force Academy. I received a standing ovation from my peers when the announcement was made during our monthly meeting. Following the meeting, one of the sergeants approached me to offer his congratulations. Then, he cautioned me that the appointment would present greater challenges.

Soon, I would come to know just what he meant.

In March, I was given a short assignment from Clark to Castle Air Force Base in California to be cross-trained in an area that specialized in the maintenance of electronic counter measures (ECM) boxes for the Boeing B-52 Stratofortress jet-powered strategic bomber aircraft. I returned from the Philippines to Travis Air Force Base in California on a Saturn Airways DC-8. Saturn was one of the commercial air carriers the military utilized to transport troops. After landing at Travis, I was able to get a seat on an Air Force C-97 Stratofreighter cargo aircraft going from Travis to Offutt Air Force Base near Omaha. I would have a few days at home before reporting to my new assignment at Castle AFB.

While in Omaha, I got to spend time with my family. My mother cooked up a special turkey dinner—something she always did on special occasions. I got to spend time with Arnie, who I continued to be proud of. He was working toward becoming a doctor. I also drove to Lincoln to visit Arlene, who by now was a junior at NU. She had been faithful to write to me often after I went in the service, and I wanted her to know just how much I appreciated it.

After a few days, I was back on a train and headed for Fresno, California, en route to Castle Air Force Base. When I checked in to my new squadron the following day, I learned that instead of attending a technical school, I would go through on-the-job training. I had a lot of free time on my hands, and spent much of it thinking about the decision I had made to attend the academy. Had it been a wise decision? I wondered.

I was nearing the point where I only had two years remaining as an enlisted airman. I reasoned that I could continue to take some off-duty college courses at Fresno State University during those final years of enlistment, and then complete my degree at the University of Nebraska, using the GI Bill to cover the cost. The idea of spending another four years at the academy, followed by serving another four or five years in the military, was becoming less and less appealing. Besides that, I still had not settled on the career path I wanted to take following graduation from the academy.

In May, I received a letter from the academy asking me to confirm my decision to accept the appointment. If I declined the appointment, the letter stated, I would not be allowed to change my mind. I'd like to say my decision was a difficult one, but in all honesty, it wasn't. Considering the reservations I'd been having, it was easy and I notified the academy that I would be declining the appointment. My decision to reject the offer was confirmed shortly after I called to tell my parents.

During the phone conversation, my mother became very quiet, as though she was disappointed in me. Three weeks later, Arnie called to say my mother had been crying for the past three days because she felt I had made a wrong decision in not accepting the appointment. Sorry to hear that I had disappointed my mother, I explained to Arnie that my decision had been made, and that I could not reverse it.

At least, that's what I thought.

I disliked that I had disappointed my mother, and wanted to do whatever I could to fix it. After praying about the situation, I decided to call the Air Force Academy. Although I had been told I could not change my mind, and calling would likely prove fruitless, I wanted to try. That way, I reasoned, I could at least tell my mother that I tried.

It was the holidays, which meant not very many people were on base. A very helpful phone operator tried unsuccessfully six times to connect me with someone who might be able to help. When we both were about ready to give up, she tried once more. This time, she got through to an Air Force captain who was part of the academy admissions office. The captain told me the admissions board would be meeting the following Monday to make the final roster for the incoming class. But he added that my chances of getting readmitted to the academy were very slim.

Over the next two days I found it difficult to sleep. But then I received the good news the day after Memorial Day, when an officer with the Air Force Academy called to say I had been readmitted to the incoming class. He called the readmission "luck." But I knew better. I knew the decision had come as a result of my mother's prayers. Both my mom and dad were excited at the news that I had been readmitted.

On June 29, 1966, I entered the Air Force Academy as a member of the Class of 1970. Of the 1,011 incoming cadets in the class, 13 were black. The first few days were devoted to a relaxed atmosphere of orientation. Then, all hell broke loose. At least that's how the cadets in training would describe the situation, as we were pretty much stripped of all privileges. I liken it to trying to drink water from a fire hose.

In a nutshell, we were introduced to military life.

I'm very tempted here to offer a blow-by-blow description of the many "abuses" we endured on the way to being transformed from civilians to tactical trained military personnel. But to do so would take up more pages here that I care to use as I share my story, and likely would be more history than anyone would care to read. Besides, I don't want to deny myself the joy of some day being able to share the details of my exciting journey, from tossing newspapers out of a wagon to flying hundreds of thousands of passengers around the world, with my grandchildren. What I will say is that the next several months played a major role in the shaping of my future, my career and my life. It was through the training I would receive, the people I would meet, and the favor I would be shown by a loving God, that I would soon become a licensed pilot.

One thing I will note, though, is that there were three events that occurred during my time in the academy that would subsequently have a lasting effect on my life.

First, was the assassination of renowned civil rights leader Dr. Martin Luther King Jr. in the spring of 1968. Dr. King was a hero to me, primarily because I agreed with his nonviolent approach to dealing with racial injustice and civil rights issues in America.

The second event was the riots that occurred in the black areas of several major United States cities during the 1960s. In Omaha, my hometown, a riot broke out during the appearance by then-presidential candidate Alabama Governor George Wallace. My hometown suffered considerable damage and destruction during that rioting. Thankfully, no one was seriously injured.

The third thing was my relationship with Dolores, whom I met during my senior year at the academy. Ours was a short courtship, but for some reason we both knew we were meant to be together. We became engaged on June 2, the night before I graduated from the academy. The next morning, during a private ceremony in which my parents, my brother Arnie and Dolores were all present, I took the oath of an officer and was commissioned as a second lieutenant in the United States Air Force. I was one of the 10 black cadets in the graduating class.

That evening I announced to my parents that Dolores and I were engaged to be married and had set a wedding date for August 1, about two weeks before I was to begin pilot training.

Flight Log: Approaching the United States

About 45 minutes after flying into Gander Center airspace, we're headed to Moncton Center in Moncton, Nova Scotia. There is a lot more chatter on the VHF radio because all inbound air traffic from Europe is being funneled into an arrival corridor near the northeastern border of the United States. This flow of air traffic is being meshed with those aircraft flying in and out of Canadian air space.

Off to my left, I can see Halifax, Nova Scotia.

The first officer and I return our international charts to our flight bags and take out the arrival charts, commonly referred to as "STARS." Although we have flown this particular trip many times and are very familiar with it, we still discuss it as though it is our first time together as a crew. Knowing my first officer will soon be elevated to captain, I feel responsible to maintain a professional image as I transition into retirement.

I keep my flight charts in several large binders in my flight bag. But I separate the charts for the arrival airport, which is Newark, and the alternate airport, which is JFK, and place them in a smaller binder. At the conclusion of the flight, I will transfer the charts from the smaller binder back to the larger one. The first officer asked if she can have my small binder at the end of our flight as a souvenir. Her request was touching. I am honored to know that a part of me will live on with the airline long after I am gone.

Moncton Center hands off our flight to Boston Center,

who in turn confirms our assigned arrival procedures after we check in. I notify the lead flight attendant that we will soon begin our descent, and that I anticipate a smooth ride. I then monitor Boston Center's frequency while the first officer issues the "goodbye" message to the passengers. Just now, Boston Center has instructed us to descend, and maintain flight level 300.

Chapter 7

Wings

Following graduation from the Air Force Academy, I began to sense the reality of the fact that I was now an officer in the United States Air Force. Reflecting on the recent events on the drive back to Omaha, I felt that I had just taken a significant step toward the promise that I had made to my new parents just after my adoption in 1955.

Dolores returned home to Washington, D.C., and began planning for our wedding. Her father had already reserved the chapel at Bolling Air Force Base, which was just a short distance from where Dolores and I had met. I remained in Omaha for the next couple of weeks, then joined Dolores in Washington. My parents planned to drive up a few days before the wedding.

I don't have to tell you who I chose to be my best man. Arnie, of course!

At noon, on August 1, Dolores and I tied the knot as we became Mr. and Mrs. Harry Arnold. We spent the next week traveling by car to upstate New York, and to Niagara Falls for our honeymoon. Then, we returned to Washington to prepare for the trip to Moody Air Force Base in Georgia, where I was to begin pilot training.

The pilot training class I was assigned to was designated 72-01, which simply meant my class would be the first to graduate from Moody AFB in the fiscal year 1972. The class was divided into two sections with 30 officers in each section. Since a majority of the officers had been part of my graduating class at the academy, I already knew several of them.

The class schedules were arranged so that while one section of the class was receiving academics in the classroom, the other section was receiving flight instructions. The class schedule for each section would flip-flop each week to assure each section of the class would receive an equal amount of morning and afternoon flying. Since the entire group of pilot candidates in the class had already accumulated approximately 30 flight hours prior to graduating, each student was scheduled to receive only enough flight hours to refresh his flying skills and then take a proficiency check ride. I received about eight hours in the aircraft before receiving my check ride.

Jim Crow Lives On

Despite all the good that was happening in my life at that time, every now and then something would happen to suddenly snap me back into reality about life, the world we live in, and the fact that I was living south of the Mason-Dixon Line.

On one occasion, I turned on the television only to see a political advertisement of an individual who was running for governor of the state of Georgia. Sitting at a desk and proudly displaying the Confederate flag in the background, this man, who I later learned was the leader of the area Ku Klux Klan, was as calm as anyone could be as he boldly invoked the "N" word on several occasions during his speech. Imagine my surprise, and my disgust. In later years, this same man, who, by the way, was not elected governor, was charged and convicted in connection with the 1958 bombing of a black church in Birmingham, Alabama, that killed several people.

The second incident happened after Dolores and I decided to move from a house trailer into an apartment in a complex where several of the pilot candidates from my class lived. Someone had told me there was an unwritten quota system for the number of blacks allowed to live in this particular complex, so I decided to get a former roommate of mine, who was white and lived in the complex, to intervene on our behalf. Roger was also a pilot candidate in my class. Roger graciously consented, went to see the apartment manager, and told him he had a friend who was looking to rent an apartment.

What Roger didn't say, though, was that his friend was black.

All the arrangements for our move to the apartment were done over the phone, so the first time the manager was aware that we were not white was when Dolores and I arrived at his office to sign the lease. At this point, the apartment manager had no other choice than to honor the lease agreement. The irony of it, though, was the fact that we were assigned an apartment next door to the only other black couple in the complex.

Training and More Training

In mid-September, I entered into the second phase of pilot training. This phase was called the primary jet phase, and we were introduced to the Cessna T-37 Tweet, a small two-pilot, twin-engine jet trainer-attack type aircraft. The aircraft was affectionately known as the "6,000-pound dog whistle" because it weighed 6,000 pounds and its two engines made a loud, high-pitched sound. I took a liking to the T-37, as well as to my instructor, Captain Crawford. Captain Crawford was a big man with an outgoing personality. He had been a T-37 instructor pilot for three years when we met, and his assignment was about to be over.

After about 15 hours of flight instruction in the T-37, I flew my first solo flight. I also flew my first spin ride, with Captain Crawford at my side. The spin maneuver was very challenging, but with Captain Crawford's help, and encouragement, I was able to execute the maneuver with little problem. I even came to like flying spins. The second phase of training also focused on instrument flying, where you learned all there is to know about Instrument Flight Rules (IFR) conditions. By the end of training in December, I knew everything there was to know about the T-37.

In early 1971, I began training in the Northrop T-38 Talon jet. Like the T-37, this was a two-seat, twin-engine aircraft, but it was a supersonic jet that was capable of flying at altitudes as high as 50,000 feet. After about 20 hours of instruction, I was flying solo.

Just prior to the end of pilot training, the members of our class received our class standings. The final class standings were based on a combination of the student's academic, flying and military grades. My class also received a list of possible aircraft choices that the Air Force was making available to us and three other undergraduate pilot training classes at different pilot training bases that were graduating during the same time period. What that meant for me, personally, was that my final grade was being compared not only with the other students in my class, but with those of the students from three other pilot training bases.

Based on my overall final grade, I requested to be a T-37 instructor pilot and was assigned to Williams Air Force Base in Phoenix. I received my Air Force pilot wings in July, and soon after headed to San Antonio for three months of flight instructor training at Randolph Air Force Base. Dolores went back to Washington, D.C., to stay with her parents while I trained. Three months later, we were back together and headed to Williams AFB and my next assignment as a flight instructor.

The brief time off gave me the opportunity to reflect on all that had happened over the past year, in particular my completing pilot and instructor training. It also gave me the opportunity to visit my parents in Omaha, whom I'd not seen since our wedding. My mind drifted back to those days, years ago, when Arnie and I were so young. We both had aspirations of growing up and becoming someone, and our parents had always supported us. Now, it appeared we both were on our way to becoming successful.

I thought about the day Arnie and I were adopted back in 1955. And I remembered how I had been just 9 years old when Arnie and I sat at the kitchen table and promised our new parents that someday the two of us would make our parents proud. Even though we were still working toward fulfilling that promise, our parents made it clear that they were already proud of us—that I had become an Air Force pilot and Arnie was now a doctor.

Establishing a Career

Once in Phoenix, we bought a 1,500-square-foot house that was still under construction. Since the house, which cost a whopping $26,000, was not going to be finished until the following month, we moved into a motel. Williams AFB was only about 30 minutes from where the new house was located, which made for an easy commute.

Shortly after we moved into our new home in January 1972, two important events occurred. First, I traded in my second lieutenant gold bars when I was promoted to first lieutenant. The second event was not as pleasant, however. Doctors had discovered that a lump in my mother's neck was cancerous. They were confident that all the cancerous cells had been removed during surgery, and that our mother would be fine, Arnie said. In late May of 1972 I received another call from my brother. He told me that the cancer had returned, and that our mother was back in the hospital. We returned to Omaha, where we visited with my mother for a few days, then returned to Phoenix. A few days later, after returning from a cross-country training flight to San Francisco, California, I drove from Williams AFB to my home in nearby Tempe. From the look on Dolores' face, I knew instantly that something was the matter. That's when she told me that my mother was gone. She had passed on Friday, shortly after I left on the flight to Riverside. But Dolores and Arnie had decided to wait until I returned to tell me.

The funeral was held the following Friday at the Sharon Seventh Day Adventist Church. Following the funeral, I remained in Omaha for a few days to help clear up some of my mother's personal affairs. In the process, I stumbled across the bankbook from the savings account my mother had opened years ago when Arnie and I were working our newspaper routes. Looking over the entries, it appeared that she had been making deposits into the bank using the money I gave her from what I earned delivering newspapers. The deposits also included the money I gave my mother when I worked summers, and money that I had been sending home since joining the military. To my surprise, it appeared she had not spent one dime of the money I had been sending her.

To this day, I don't know what she intended to do with that money, which had earned considerable interest. Maybe she was saving it for her grandchildren. I do know that I was very touched by the fact that she would hold onto the money, despite the fact that she probably could have used it.

Over the next few days, my thought gravitated more toward my father. At 74, I wondered how he would fare on his own. Sure, he was still very active in church, and he was an avid bowler. I knew I didn't have to worry much about his welfare, but after being with my mom for nearly 50 years, I'm sure there would be many periods of loneliness. I just had to trust God to see him through those times.

Another thing that tugged at me was the remembrance of my birth mother, Charlita, and the tragedy that had befallen our family, beginning with her death at age 30. I wondered why she was killed at such a young age, and why my adoptive mother, who had just recently turned 62, had now been taken away from me. It had been my hope that someday my children would have the privilege of spending time with their grandmother—sitting on her lap while she imparted words of wisdom from God's Word to them.

In early 1973, I enrolled in night courses at Arizona State University in Tempe, seeking a master's degree in political science. In June of that year, I was promoted to captain. The promotion was a big deal, and one that I really excited about. But nothing excited me more the news I received six months later, when Dolores called me at work one day in January 1974 to announce that she was pregnant. The doctors had set her due date at September 6.

A lot took place in my career between then and the day our first child was born. But nothing brought me more excitement than the joy of knowing I was about to become a daddy—that we were going to be parents.

Dolores and I took Lamaze birthing classes together and it was official that I would be allowed in the delivery room. For some time, we had "labored" over what we would name the baby. It had come down to Alicia and Camille. We made the decision just a couple of days before the baby was born, after someone had commented that I resembled the comedian Bill Cosby. Cosby's wife's name is Camille.

Finally, the big day arrived!

At 8:30 p.m. on September 2, 1974 (Labor Day), we welcomed our beautiful young daughter, Camille Elisabeth Arnold, into the world. By the way, the middle name of Elisabeth was her maternal grandmother's first name.

I saw much change in my career over the next couple of years, leading up to my eventual decision to leave the military.

My tour of duty as an instructor pilot was scheduled to end December 1975 and, though I enjoyed my job as a training instructor, and had hoped to go on to become a fighter pilot, I knew the likelihood of that happening was not very good. With the war in Vietnam winding down, there were certain to be severe cutbacks in available flying assignments. Many of the pilots due for reassignment would be reassigned to nonflying assignments known as rated supplement jobs. Taking a pilot out of a flying job was akin to a death sentence for the pilot's career.

When I came up for my reassignment from Williams AFB, there were a total of 250 pilots up for reassignment throughout the different Air Force commands and only 50 fifty flying positions available. To fill those spots, the Air Force Personnel Center would review the files of each of the 250 pilots, considering all their accomplishments. Those not selected would be given what was known as "rated supplemental assignments." There were no fighter pilot positions included in the 50 jobs available, which made the position less attractive to me. Still, I was very pleased to learn that I had been assigned to one of the flying jobs.

As one of the top four pilots on the list, I was assigned to the Military Airlift Command flying C-141 cargo airplanes, and assigned to McGuire Air Force Base in New Jersey. However, after reviewing my records, the Military Airlift Command reassigned me to the 93rd Medical Evacuation Squadron at Scott Air Force Base in Illinois, where I would be flying the C-9, a military version of the DC-9 airliner. This was considered a choice assignment. As a perk for me, Scott AFB was located just across the Missouri River from St. Louis, where my brother, Arnie, was living.

I felt like I had been truly blessed.

Our home in Tempe sold quickly, and we packed up and moved to O'Fallon, Illinois, which was a few miles from Scott AFB. While I spent a short while in Long Beach, California, doing my initial flight safety simulator training for the C-9, Dolores and Camille lived with my wife's parents in Washington. We moved into our new home in O'Fallon when I returned from Long Beach.

A Love for the People

I began working with the C-9 Squadron, whose job it was to transport Department of Defense personnel who were receiving medical treatment to and from cities throughout the United States. A typical mission would include flights into military and civilian airports. During my initial simulator training, my instructor had emphasized the necessity of flying the aircraft in a smooth manner because on many of my missions I would be transporting critically ill patients. The C-9 maintained a crew of seven people in addition to the aircraft commander: two co-pilots, two nurses, 2 medical technicians and a flight mechanic. On occasion, a doctor would accompany a critically ill patient on a flight. The plane was configured to carry up to 40 ambulatory patients and 33 patients on litters. The front section of the aircraft was the critical care section, equipped with enough medical supplies for a doctor to perform an emergency surgery were it necessary.

Flying the C-9 was very special to me. I cared for all of my passengers, but children with serious illnesses or injuries especially tugged at my heart. I was also sensitive to those passengers with burn wounds.

A few months after joining the C-9 Squadron, I was upgraded to the position of Aircraft Commander.

Sometimes on my off days, my family and I would drive across the Missouri River to St. Louis to spend some time with Arnie and his family. At other times, they would come to visit us. During one of their visits, I secured a flight line pass for Arnie and took him to see a C-9. I took him to the cockpit and let him sit in the captain's seat. By the big smile on my brother's face, one would have thought that he had just been given a million dollars.

Time for More Change

Although the mission of the C-9 was dynamic and the flying was great, it was becoming apparent that the time I was spending away from my family was putting a strain on our marriage. I needed to do something to fix that.

On several of my missions, I was paired with a pilot from the C-9 Associate Reserve Squadron. In addition to flying C-9 missions, many of these pilots were full time airline pilots who worked for commercial airlines. When I first became part of the C-9 squadron, the thought of flying for a commercial airline was the furthest thing from my mind. But now I found myself willing to entertain the idea, especially if it could, in some way, help ease the problems in my marriage.

My commitment to the Air Force was not scheduled to end until April 1977, but I thought I'd do some initial investigation just to see if flying commercial was something I might enjoy. Eventually, I submitted applications to several airlines. Near the end of 1976, I received a call from American Airlines asking me to come to Chicago, Illinois, for an interview. Following my initial interview with American, I was informed that I had been medically disqualified for a pilot's position. This was news to me, as I was not aware of any medical problems. American never disclosed what the medical problem was, either.

Just as I was about to close the door on any chance of my ever flying with a commercial airline, I received a call from Continental Airlines. The next day, I flew from St. Louis to Los Angeles for an interview. What was interesting about the call from Continental was the fact they the company had not hired any new pilots in five years. The interview lasted all day, and concluded with a complete physical examination. A few days later, I got a call from Continental notifying me that I had been accepted for the initial hiring class, which would start in January 1977.

Because of a few complications, and about a yard of red tape, I was not able to obtain my release from the Air Force in time to make the first or second hiring classes at Continental. According to my squadron commander, my official date of department from the Air Force was not until April. To allow me to leave any sooner would be setting precedent that others might want to take advantage of.

Though bothered by that decision, I decided to use my accrued leave time and went on active terminal leave from the Air Force from February until April in order to make the third starting class at Continental. Meanwhile, I received calls from two others airlines, which I graciously declined.

In February, we sold our house in O'Fallon and I drove Dolores and Camille to Washington to, once again, take up residence with Dolores' parents. Only this time, my assignment wasn't with the military. It was with Continental.

Flight Log: The Descent

Most pilots will tell you the workload on the flight deck increases once you begin your descent from cruising altitude for the arrival at the destination airport. The aircraft goes from a moderate amount of air traffic control activity at the higher altitudes to an area where there is a heavy amount of activity at the lower altitudes. This is especially true when an aircraft is descending to lower altitudes in the northeastern portion of the United States.

We had commenced our "before descent checklist" when we initially started our descent from 34,000 to 30,000 feet. It's especially important that we check and confirm that the correct altitude was set in the altitude selector window when the aircraft was assigned a new altitude by air traffic control. An incorrect altitude setting could spoil your entire day.

Our flight path will carry us over Bangor, Maine, in the northeastern portion of the United States, then over Vermont, and on past Massachusetts. As we approach flight level 300, Boston Center directs us to continue our descent to flight level 240. The present Newark weather is pretty much the same as the weather forecast that we had received prior to our departure from London, unlike previous flights where there had been significant wind shifts at the Newark airport that required a change in the direction for planes taking off and landing. If a flight's arrival time places the flight in the middle of a runway change the flight can be placed in a holding pattern for up to a half hour. But there are no such problems today.

Boston Center finally hands us off to New York Center as the aircraft crosses over into New York Center's airspace. I give a long sigh, and smile as I think about a joke I once heard growing up.

"What did the dog say when he backed into a fan?" the man asked.

"I don't know. What?"

"It won't be long now."

Chapter 8

The Airlines: Part 1

I allowed myself three days travel time for the drive from St. Louis to Los Angeles, figuring it would give me a full day to familiarize myself with the area around the Continental Training Center. My hotel, the Hacienda, was only about 15 minutes away from the center.

Training class consisted of 18 new hires, most of whom were former military—either from the Air Force, Marines or Navy. The others had worked as general aviation pilots. At age 31, I was among the oldest in a class that ranged in age from 24 to 35. There were also two white females in the class, Continental's first. I was one of only two blacks. We were told the airline had decided to hire 80 pilots from its list of 10,000 applicants. I learned that I ranked number 1,127 on the Continental seniority list. I was also told that prior to 1997, only three black pilots had been hired by Continental since the mid to late 1960s. With the hiring of one black in the first class in 1977, and two in my class, that brought the total number of black pilots on Continental's seniority list to six.

For most of the next six weeks, all our waking hours were spent learning the ins and outs of the Boeing 727, a midsized, three-engine plane that carried about 150 passengers. It was the plane we would eventually be assigned to as second officers, once training ended and we graduated. The second officer was basically a flight engineer whose responsibility was to ride alongside the pilot and co-pilot and monitor the plane's systems. While the work was fun and exciting, the pay as a first-year pilot wasn't anything to write home about. In fact, at $1,000 a month, I was earning only about a third of what I was paid as an Air Force pilot.

Near the end of training, I turned down an offer to remain in Los Angeles to be a second-officer training instructor because I wanted to become more experienced at line flying. I had learned my initial base assignment for Continental would be in Texas, and was given a choice of being assigned to El Paso or Houston. I chose Houston.

There were 32 Continental flight crews assigned to the Houston base. During my first two months there, I flew reserve status. In June 1977, I was awarded my first regular flying schedule. That month my flight schedule consisted of 12 night turns between Houston and Los Angeles, which amounted to all-night flights. The trips were divided into three sets of four consecutive days of flying, with 18 days off. That may sound like a lot of free time, but when you consider what took place on the backside—three periods of consecutive flying over four days—you can easily see the need for rest.

For a brief time after arriving in Houston, I explored the possibility of continuing my military career by joining a flying squadron in either the Air Force Reserves or in the National Guard. While there did exist the possibility of my doing so, the various time constraints didn't work with my desire to strengthen my relationship with Continental and I was forced to abandon the idea.

During that period, Continental found itself in the midst of a pilot hiring boom, with a majority of its new hires being assigned to the Houston base. In August 1977, I was selected by the chief pilot to become the second officer check airman for the Houston base. My duties included flying 25 hours of Initial Operating Experience (IOE) training and administering yearly check rides with incoming second officers.

In November 1977, I, along with five other black pilots in the Houston area, three of whom were flying for Texas International Airlines, came together to form the Southwest Chapter of the Organization of Black Airline Pilots (OBAP). Nationally, there were several chapters of OBAP with a total membership of about 100 black pilots. Of the nearly 40,000 commercial pilots then flying for scheduled airlines, only 250 were black. The focus of OBAP was to inform and encourage minority youths about possible careers in aviation. I was selected as the treasurer for the Southwest chapter.

Ebony Magazine, one of the nation's most popular black publications during that time, did a feature article on black airline pilots in its January 1978 edition.

One of the highlights of that time happened in March 1978, when members of OBAP were invited to speak to students at some of the area high schools in Houston during Career Day. During my appearance at one of the schools I met and befriended a young man named Ron McNair, who was a black astronaut based at the Houston Space Center. Ron had just recently been selected to the prestigious position of astronaut. On January 28, 1986, he and six other crew members died when the space shuttle they were aboard exploded seconds after launch.

There were a number of things I came to know about McNair after his death—things that caused me to have even more respect for my fellow pilot than before. For instance, in the summer of 1959, when he was just 9 years old, McNair refused to leave a segregated public library without being allowed to check out his books. After the police and his mother were called, he was allowed to borrow books from the library—which now bears his name. A children's book, titled *Ron's Big Mission,* gives a fictionalized account of this event.

McNair was valedictorian of his high school in 1967, graduated magna cum laude from the North Carolina A&T State University in Greensboro with an undergraduate degree in engineering physics, and got his Ph.D. in physics from the prestigious Massachusetts Institute of Technology. In 1978, he became one of only 35 applicants selected from a pool of 10,000 for the NASA astronaut program and subsequently became the second African

American chosen to fly in space.

By April 1978, my seniority had reached the point where I could fly as a first officer or co-pilot on the Boeing 727—an opportunity I quickly took advantage of. Being first officer meant I would be flying on reserve status, but it was still better than flying as a second officer. In late spring, I went to Los Angeles for simulator training, then went to Phoenix for the aircraft portion of the training. By early summer, I was back in Houston and flying as a first officer on the Boeing 727.

Continental Airlines continued to grow at a phenomenal rate in 1978-79. At one point, five of my classmates from the 17th Squadron at the Air Force Academy were flying for Continental.

In the fall of 1978, a major event happened that would have a lasting effect on the airline industry. That was when the United States government decided to disband the Civil Aeronautics Board (CAB), the government agency charged with regulating the airline industry. The result of such a decision, in effect, meant that where they had been prohibited from doing so before, airlines could now start up and stop routes between any two cities in the United States. As a result, analysts predicted that small and midsized airlines would be taken over by the major airlines.

That would include Continental which, at that time, was considered a midsized airline. These same analysts predicted that in 20 to 30 years the airline industry as a whole would consist of only three major airlines: American, Delta and United.

The full effect of deregulation became obvious in 1979, as mergers began taking place between various airlines. Some airlines even filed for bankruptcy. A downturn in the nation's economy further complicated matters. Some airlines, Continental being one of them, suffered a huge loss of revenue when all its DC-10 aircraft were grounded after the crash of an American Airlines DC-10 in Chicago, Illinois. The DC-10 was Continental's only long-haul aircraft, and routes to Hawaii and Australia were severely impacted.

Suddenly, the word "furlough," which in airline circles was

considered as the dreaded "F" word, had descended on all airlines.

A New Addition to the Family

In spite of the fact that my future as an airline pilot appeared to be in jeopardy, there were some good things going on in my life.

In March 1979, Dolores and I began adoption proceedings in hopes of adding a second child to our family. Camille was already 5 years old, and we wanted her to have a sibling, in this case a brother, to grow up with. It was also at this time that we began looking to become more involved in church and connected with a local church in Houston.

My father passed away in June of that year at the age of 81.

In August, Dolores and I learned that we had been accepted into the adoption program and the adoption agency already had a baby boy picked out for us. On the day of the adoption, we arrived at the agency and were ushered into a waiting room. A few minutes later, our new son was brought into the room. At first glance, Dolores and I knew he was our child—our son!

We named him Corben Eugene Arnold.

The first name was derived from the biblical name Corban, which means "given to God." Eugene was the middle name of his maternal grandfather.

He was born on March 24, and was now five months old.

A few weeks later, Corben and Camille were part of the first baby dedication ceremony to be held at Northfield Christian Outreach Center.

Over the next year, the furloughs at Continental continued, but at a slower pace. Even though the furloughs meant that I would have to return to the second-officer position on the Boeing 727, I still considered myself fortunate because some of my friends from the Air Force and the academy, who had been hired by Continental in 1978 and in early 1979, had been furloughed.

In late 1980, we sold our home and moved to Reston, Virginia. It was a good move for the family for a number of reasons, including the fact that our children would now be closer to their grandparents. As for my work, I would commute back and forth to Houston when I was scheduled to fly.

Texas Interrnational was merged with Continental in 1982, and relocated its headquarters from Los Angeles to Houston. The company retained the name Continental.

The merger created a whirlwind of controversy, particularly with the pilots from both airlines. For one thing, the merger resulted in the creation of a new seniority list, which pushed some pilots further down on the list than they had been previously. There was also growing tension between the new Continental management team and the labor unions at Continental over labor contracts. The company CEO had been demanding wage cuts from the unions, even prior to the merger. A major battle was brewing, and it appeared that the situation at Continental would be a litmus test for the entire airline industry. There was a feeling among the Continental pilots that our pilot group would come out on the short end of the stick.

There had been rumors that something major was about to happen at Continental. And on September 23, 1983, I was flying the last flight of a three-day trip from San Francisco when I received a transmission from Houston Flight Operations saying Continental had filed for bankruptcy.

I'm not an expert on what takes place when a business files for bankruptcy, but if the scene at the Houston terminal over the next 24 hours was any indication, it's not a pretty sight.

After landing in Houston, the captain had to wait for ground personnel to marshal the aircraft into its assigned gate. He told the crew members to take all our personal belongings from the crew rooms because the building would be locked once the final Houston-bound flight arrived. Naturally, the mood in the crew room was somewhat somber. The question on everyone's mind was: What now?

Knowing I would not be able to fly home on Continental, once in my hotel I phoned Eastern Airlines reservations and listed myself as a "space available" passenger on one of their flights.

I always kept a valid pass on another airline as a backup, just in case I couldn't get a seat on a Continental flight. The next morning, when I took the hotel van to Terminal B to check in for my Eastern flight, I noticed all the doors to Continental's Terminal C were locked. I also noticed a large number of Continental aircraft parked on the airport ramp. It was a sight that would not fade from my memory for many years to come. During my layover after flying Eastern from Houston to Atlanta, I saw a flight crew from a Continental flight walking down the concourse. They had been stranded in Boston, they said, when Continental ceased flight operations. They said Eastern had given seats to the entire crew for the flight back to Houston.

On that day, when Continental officially filed for bankruptcy, the airline announced its plan was to ease operations for two days, and reduce its workforce from 12,000 to 4,000 when it resumed operations. Not many options were available for me regarding work as a pilot, though I did explore the possibility of going to work for People Express, a smaller airline that several of my associates had connected with.

In early 1984, I returned to work for what was now called the "New Continental." As I recall, the only resemblance it had to the former airline was the name and the color of the aircraft. Unlike the former airline, the new setting was very unsettling. Very stressful! I recall someone once describing the atmosphere and environment as "us against the world." Although I returned to work in my same position as a second office line check airman, my pay had been cut in half and my monthly flying hours had been increased. Several times I thought about resigning, but I had made a decision and was determined to stick it out.

As the "New Continental" began to expand and grow, I was awarded a captain slot on the Boeing 727. Because my commuting flight schedule from Washington, D.C. to Houston had become more strenuous under the new Continental work rules, we decided to sell our home in Reston and move back to Houston. We also reconnected with our former church, Northfield Christian Outreach Center, where we enrolled Camille and Corben in the

Christian school.

In early 1985, Continental issued a pilot system bid indicating that it would be soon be adding new Boeing 737-300 aircraft to its fleet. The aircraft would be the first of Boeing's Classic series of medium-range, narrow-bodied jetliners. The new aircraft would be based in Denver and Houston. I had always desired to live in the Denver area, so this was perfect. I submitted a bid and was soon notified that I had been awarded a captain position at the Denver base. We moved to Denver in late May

The move to Denver was good for my family in more than one way.

As had been a main focus for us as a family, we immediately began searching for a church after we were settled into our new home, and settled in at Happy Church, where Wallace and Marilyn Hickey were the pastors. We had become familiar with Marilyn Hickey's ministry some years earlier when she held a women's meeting in the Houston area. At that meeting, I had been asked to serve as an usher. During the service, Marilyn pointed me out and called me up front. She then spoke prophetically over me and gave me a piece of paper with the Scripture verse Luke 21:15 written on it. I later read the verse, which said: "For I will give you a mouth and wisdom, which all your adversaries shall not be able to gainsay nor resist." It would be years before the reality of that verse would become meaningful to me, but since that time those words have played a major role in my life, my spiritual development and my career.

I completed training to fly the Boeing 737-300 in October 1985. Since I would now be based out of Denver, I would no longer have to commute back to Houston. My daughter had won a position on the community summer swim team shortly after our move to the area known as Highlands Ranch, and my having to commute had caused me to miss all her swim competitions. I vowed to never allow that to happen again.

Eventually, things worked out well for my family and me. When I was not flying during the summer, I was able to attend my daughter's swimming meets, and served as an assistant coach with Corben's Little League baseball team. I was also able to become more involved as a volunteer worker in church.

The year 1986 brought with it several events that would have a long-term effect on me, as well as on Continental Airlines.

On January 28, 1986, the space shuttle Challenger exploded shortly after takeoff and the entire crew died. A few days before the launch of the Challenger, I had seen that my friend Ron McNair was a member of the shuttle crew. His sudden death, as well as the others, was devastating.

In June, Continental finally emerged from its initial filing of Chapter 11 bankruptcy which, though it seemed like a lifetime ago, had taken place only three years before in September 1983.

In September, Texas Air Corporation acquired People Express and Frontier Airlines. People Express had previously purchased Frontier Airlines in the fall of 1985. The addition of People Express meant that Newark, New Jersey, would now be a pilot base and the Boeing 747 would be added to the aircraft fleet. The addition of Frontier Airlines meant that the Boeing 737-200 would now be part of the aircraft fleet.

In February 1987, Texas Air merged one of its subsidiaries, New York Air, into Continental. New York Air's main pilot base was at New York's LaGuardia Airport. The positive aspect of this merger was that, with the addition of People Express, Continental would have a strong presence in the New York metropolitan area. The negative aspect was Continental's new responsibility of managing the flight operations of yet another airline, which proved to be overwhelming to the extent that Continental was eventually forced to retrench and post pilot reduction bids—a move that resulted in the furloughing of pilots.

The following year, I decided to move my family into a larger home in the Highlands Ranch area. My daughter was entering her freshman year of high school, and my son was now in the fourth grade. I felt that my family was now ready for a larger home. It was during Mother's Day weekend that my wife and I found our new home. We decided to rent out our former home when we moved into our new home.

In 1988, I was offered the position of assistant chief pilot for the Boeing 737-300. Not wanting to compromise the stability I had been able to develop with my family and church, I turned down the offer. My wife and I became leaders of a cell group for Happy Church, and hosted a weekly meeting in our home. Camille enjoyed hosting a similar Bible study for the youth, as well. We had begun to establish some good, godly relationships, and I didn't want to do anything that could possibly interrupt what I knew the Lord was doing in our lives.

The downturn in the economy and the retrenchment of Continental continued into 1990. There were also some milestones that occurred during that year.

In August, Dolores and I celebrated 20 years of marriage by taking a weeklong vacation to Maui. It would be our first extended vacation since the birth of our daughter. A couple of months later, we attended my 20th class reunion at the Air Force Academy. It was the first time I had seen many of my classmates since graduation.

In December 1990, Continental filed bankruptcy for a second time. The airline was still continuing to retrench and to seek a positive cash flow position. The mergers had brought with them a large number of different types of aircraft with some steep lease rates and maintenance costs.

In February 1991, Continental unveiled its new branding—blue and gold livery and the globe logo. While the new exterior paint scheme was refreshing, the bottom line was the number of passengers Continental was attracting. Over the next two years, the airline continued to retrench and find its place in the ever-evolving airline industry. Two years later, Continental emerged from bankruptcy with financial help from Air Canada, Air Partners and Texas Pacific Group.

Camille graduated with honors from Highlands Ranch High School in June, and would enroll at Oral Roberts University in Tulsa, Oklahoma, in the fall. Corben was about to start his freshman year at Highlands Ranch High.

A Breakup of a Different Kind

In 1994, Continental named a new CEO. Over the next two years, he would be instrumental in bringing about a positive change in the attitude of Continental's employees, and a change in the perception of the airline in the eyes of the public. Continental closed its Denver base in October, but expanded bases in Newark, New Jersey; and Houston, and opened a new base in Greensboro, North Carolina. Rather than relocate my family for what seemed like the hundreth time, I chose to remain in Denver and commute to either Houston or Newark.

While my decision to remain in Denver was made primarily with my family's interests at heart, that decision alone didn't solve some of the other problems that had been brewing between Dolores and me. In early 1995, we came to the amicable decision to file for separation after 24 years of marriage.

Since early childhood, my life had seen a number of devastating moments. But the breakup of my marriage was one of—if not the darkest—times of my life. It was topped only by the deaths of my mother and my adoptive parents.

As part of the divorce decree, I was awarded sole physical custody of Corben who, at the time, was having some problems in school. I was fortunate to have the friendship of a couple that lived in our community, and a couple from church, both of whom were especially helpful in caring for my son when I needed to be out of town for work.

Camille remained with her mom, but we maintained a great relationship as she grew older.

I would love to say that, despite the divorce, my relationship with my children was not greatly affected. Unfortunately, it was just the opposite—especially with Corben.

During the separation, I moved back into the previous house we owned in Denver that we had been renting out. When the divorce became final, I considered moving to Newark and taking Corben with me. The problem was that it not only would interrupt Corben's schooling, but he would be forced to make other adjustments as well. I decided to stay in Denver and familiar surroundings. To minimize my time away from Corben, I would bid trips that had Denver layovers.

Now that I was divorced, my relationship with my children was even more important, and came second only to my personal relationship with the Lord. The divorce had put my relationship with my children in disarray, and I realized that I needed to do everything possible to rectify the situation. Part of that was doing what was best for my son.

It was at that point that I began to see a dim light at the end of the tunnel. Or was it a train coming from the opposite direction?

Flight Log: Changing Landscape

As we continue our descent into the New York/New Jersey area, I allow myself a moment to reflect on a few things. My first thought is that I have no real complaints for what I have experienced during my career at Continental. What more could I ask for? Perhaps a few more years in the left seat. Maybe that the retirement age for commercial pilots could be raised to 65. Then again, I feel blessed to have flown as a captain for the past 22 years.

I wonder what will be my legacy at Continental.

In thinking back over the years here, I can't remember any major incidents with other crewmembers. There had been the potential for major problems to develop on a few occasions, but they were always averted. I had managed to diffuse the situations before they escalated into something significant.

I think about the years I flew as second officer, and then as first officer, and some of the captains I have flown with. I learned something from each of them—some of the rules of etiquette you might say. Some things I learned were good, some not so good. But they all served a purpose, and they all served to make me a better captain, and pilot.

One thing I learned early in my career was that certain topics discussed within the confines of the cockpit, which won't be mentioned here, were taboo because they had the potential of becoming volatile very quickly and could lead to a strained relationship between crew members. The last thing that a captain needed was to have an adversarial relationship with his first officer during an aircraft emergency.

Another thing I was taught was the captain was never to allow another crew member set the tone or the atmosphere on the flight deck. Setting the tone was the sole responsibility of the captain. A third thing I recalled was that not everyone on the crew was going to like you. As with any profession, pilots are made up of individuals with all types of beliefs and upbringings. Many of these beliefs have been formed over many years and are not subject to change.

When I was flying as a first officer, for instance, a captain decided it was necessary that I know his position on the flight, and in the cockpit.

"When I am on the flight deck, I just want to have a working relationship with the other flight crew members," he told me. Then he told me that I wasn't there to ask him to invite me to dinner or to ask his permission to date his daughter.

Where did that come from?

I know, and I'm pretty sure most people reading this will know too.

Needless to say, the two of us never became good friends.

There was one captain who epitomized what I considered all the good traits in a captain. I had flown with Bill as his second and first officer. Over time, we were separated as we were assigned to separate bases, but we stayed in touch. I attended Bill's retirement party almost 10 years ago. It is no coincidence that Bill will be attending mine in just a few short hours.

I think about the fact that Bill had graduated from the United States Military Academy, and I was an Air Force Academy graduate, and the Air Force-Army football game that's schedule to be played this evening. Glacing over at my first officer, I am pleased that Continental has hired a number of female pilots during my years with the airline, and that I have flown with a number of them. As a minority, I am also glad that Continental has addressed the diversity issue while

I was at the airline. I was one of the first blacks to be hired at Continental and one of the first blacks to pilot a Boeing 777 as a captain there. Continental had done well regarding the hiring of minorities, and that pleased me. But truthfully, as with most every other airline, and business for that matter, there is still so much room for improvement.

One final part of the diversity issue I had hoped to see before retirement was the hiring of a black female pilot. It hasn't happened yet, as I prepare to enter into retirement, so it won't happen before I do.

I'm told that a number of black female pilots are currently being interviewed for future new hire classes. I feel very strongly about the minority issue, and believe that more exposure and more information are the keys to enticing more minorities to enter the field of aviation. For years, I've made a point of visiting the inner city grade schools and high schools during career days. Maybe some of those visits are about to pay off.

Chapter 9

The Airlines: Part 2

During the summer of 1995, I was one of two passengers flying standby on a fight from Newark to Denver. When the ticket agent called my name, along with that of another passenger, I noticed a beautiful woman as she approached the podium for her seat assignment. I soon learned that she was the other standby passenger on the flight to Denver. We greeted one another while standing at the ticket desk, then continued our conversation as we proceeded down the jetway leading to the aircraft.

Interestingly enough, we discovered the ticket agent had assigned both of us seats in first class, and that we were sitting directly across the aisle from each other.

She introduced herself as Christine, and said she worked in the flight attendants' administration office at Continental's Denver base. She was returning from visiting her daughter, Kym, and son-in-law, Rick, and her their 2-year-old daughter, Morgan. Morgan was Christine's first grandchild, and it quickly became obvious that she was definitely fond of her. In fact, we spent a majority of the flight talking about little Morgan, and looking at pictures of her, Kym and Rick. Before we landed in Denver, Christine and I exchanged phone numbers and promised to keep in touch. Over the next few months we grew closer, although neither of us was ready for a serious relationship. My recent divorce was still fresh on my mind. Still, we developed a very good friendship. In fact, Christine offered to be a backup contact for my son when I was away on a trip.

Corben's school situation at school continued to deteriorate, to the point, in fact, that he had become pretty much isolated from the other students. I desperately needed to find a solution, or my son was in jeopardy of not completing his junior year in high school.

The solution to my problem was beyond anything I could have ever imagined.

While discussing the situation with Christine, she offered to sell me her home in Aurora. She said she would be willing to transfer to Continental's reservation center in Houston.

I was surprised at the suggestion, especially considering what Christine would be giving up to move to Houston. She had very strong connections to Aurora, including the fact that she had served as a city commissioner there. She was very happy living there. At first, I tried to talk her out of it. But I quickly learned that when Christine makes up her mind about something there is no talking her out of it.

In January 1996, both our homes sold. I helped Christine move to her new home in Houston, and I moved into her former home in Aurora. The move to Aurora came just in time for Corben to start the second semester of his junior year at Gateway High School in Aurora. I spent the first few months helping Corben settle into his new school, and preparing for baseball season. I also stayed in close touch with Christine, who was adjusting well in Houston.

Shortly after moving to Aurora, I connected with Heritage Christian Center, a multicultural church where Bishop Dennis Leonard was pastor. Sitting under Bishop Leonard's teaching and attending certain developmental classes, including a layman's counseling course, were of great help enabling me to confront and deal with some of the issues and mistakes of my past. Interestingly enough, Christine's major in college was counseling and came in very handing as she provided strong input in helping me to deal with some of those issues.

Corben had a good second semester at school, and he had

a successful season playing baseball. In May, Camille came to live with us during summer break from ORU. It was good to see that she and Corben had time together. Christine continued to be part of our lives, helping Camille acquire an internship with a local TV station in Aurora for the summer. Camille returned to school in the fall to begin her senior year, and Corben started his senior year at Gateway High. While Camille was excelling at ORU, I was pleased to learn that Corben had turned a similar corner in high school.

During a conference I had with the school counselor at Gateway High, I learned that Corben was excelling in all his classes and was on track to graduate on time. Sitting there listening to the counselor's comments about my son, it occurred to me that those same words could just as easily have been applied to me. I had wanted to desperately to be a positive influence on both my children, and now it seemed I was getting what I had been believing God for. Some of my good traits were finally rubbing off on my son.

In addition to his improvement in the classroom, Corben had also excelled during the baseball season. In fact, he received a baseball scholarship to a junior college in Kansas.

In early May 1997, Camille graduated with honors from ORU, something her mother and I were very proud of. The next month, my friend Rick and I loaded up a U-Haul truck with furniture, hooked up Camille's car to the rear, and Camille and I drove to Fort Worth, Texas, where she had accepted a job at Kenneth Copeland Ministries. I spend the next few days unloading furniture and helping set up Camille's new apartment before returning to Denver.

Any father reading this will attest to the fact that leaving a child to fend for himself or herself is tough enough, but it's especially difficult when it's your daughter. In this case, it was my only daughter. But I quickly found solace in knowing that Camille would be fine—that she would not be alone and uncared for. Not long after she was settled in, Camille informed me that her new boss had just moved to Texas from North Carolina.

Ron Jordan and his wife, Edna, who had four children of their own, quickly took to Camille and "adopted" her as one of their own. They assured Dolores and me that they would watch over our child and make sure she stayed safe during her transition period. To this day, I'm pleased to say, even though Camille is now married and a mother herself, she remains as much a part of the Jordan's family as she does ours.

A Time of Reflection

After returning to Denver from Fort Worth, I decided to take a few days to rest. It had been a very difficult two years for me since the divorce. I thought about the many kind people who had helped me, both spiritually and emotionally, to get through that time. Of course, the One who was the most influential was Jesus Christ. Admittedly, there were times when I had to fight hard to stay in faith—to the truth that God would bring me through. There were times, for instance, when I would be awakened in the middle of the night wondering, *Lord, why me?* The odd thing is that seemingly every time I would have that thought, I could sense the Lord answering right back to me, *Why not you.*

Camille and Corben were very instrumental in helping me through that period of my life as well. They gave me a purpose in life. I knew that children of divorced parents go through a lot of mixed feelings. It's a known fact that when divorce happens, one of the first questions that comes to mind for the children was whether the breakup was their fault. Not only did I want to dispel such a thought in my children's minds, but I also wanted to be available to lend support to both of them.

Thirdly, there was Christine, who was always very giving and supportive of me every step along the way.

There were others whose kindness impacted me in one way or another, including friends like Jim and Sandy, Rodney and Yolanda, my buddy Rick, and a few of my former classmates from the Air Force academy: Reuben, Norman, Othe and Dorsey. Along the way there were others who spoke into my life, or provided wise counsel when I really needed it. And I will forever be grateful to each of them.

In late August 1997, Corben enrolled at Central Junior College in Pearson, Kansas—a bright spot in both our lives. With Corben now away at school, and Camille started on her career path, I now felt more of a freedom to extend my boundaries regarding flights. In the fall, I decided to bid off the Boeing 737 aircraft and bid onto the Boeing 757-200. The Boeing 757-200, which was a 178-passenger aircraft, gave me the flexibility of being able to fly long-haul domestic trips, or to Europe and the Caribbean. Not long after that, I completed my training as a captain and began flying to countries like England, Ireland, Germany, Portugal and Santo Domingo.

In 1999, Continental initiated nonstop service on the Boeing 757-200 from Cleveland, Ohio, to London's Gatwick International Airport. I decided to bid this trip series because it made my commute from Denver to Newark a little easier, and I would get the opportunity to fly into the city of London for the first time. Eventually, I was flying to cities like Zurich, Switzerland and to the South American city of Sao Paulo, Brazil; to Santo Domingo; and the Dominican Republic.

During the summer of 2000, I attended Christine's family reunion in St. Louis, Missouri, my first opportunity to meet her family. That same year, Christine retired from Continental. Rick, my long-time buddy, also hung up his wings that year, but not by choice. Sixty was the mandatory retirement age for commercial airline pilots, and Rick had reached that milestone. Though there was no fanfare surrounding his departure, Rick told me later that he flew the three-day Newark to London Gatwick Airport trip for his retirement flight and that his father, who had never flown before, was on the flight.

Over the last couple of years I had taken an interest in motorcycles, thanks to Rick, who himself was an enthusiast. By the spring of 2001, I had tested enough Harley-Davidsons that I was ready to own one and purchased a new Harley-Davidson Wide Glide. Anyone who knows anything about Harleys knows it can take forever to get one of these amazing machines. I had ordered a 2000 model the year before, but the waiting list was so long that it took well over a year for my name to reach the top of the list. By the time my name reached the top of the dealer's list, the 2001 models were out.

A New Life Dawns

In July 2001, having come to grips with a number of things that had plagued me over the past several years, I decided to turn a new corner and start life anew. I asked Christine to marry me, and she said yes. On November 24, Christine and I were married during a lovely ceremony at the Crystal Rose Palace in Denver. Kym, Christine's daughter, was maid of honor, and Arnie was my best man (for the second time). Camille was among the bridesmaids and Corben was a groomsman. Christine's son, Kevin, walked his mother down the aisle.

A few days after the wedding, I was scheduled to make a six-day trip that included flights to Hawaii, Guam and Tokyo. Though it was not our "official" honeymoon, Christine and I took advantage of the opportunity to visit some historic sites and enjoy some delectable food. It was exciting for the two of us, for instance, that one night we were able to celebrate at a restaurant in Guam, and the next night have dinner in Honolulu and walk along the sands of Waikiki Beach. Over the next several months, Christine would accompany me on flights to places like Frankfurt, Germany; Zurich, Switzerland; and London.

In the spring of 2002, we both sold our homes in Pennsylvania and Aurora and moved to Parker, a suburb of Denver. Around that same time, I made one final career decision and chose to train on the Boeing 777-200, a new aircraft Continental had acquired. My main concern in switching to a new, larger aircraft was in the fact that I would be trying to learn a new aircraft at such a late stage in my career. I thought about the amount of study time I would have to devote for a new aircraft. Because of my love for flying, I put my all into knowing everything there was to know about the planes I flew. I became totally immersed in my training classes because it was my purpose to know my new aircraft as well as I knew the back of my hand.

After spending some time in prayer, and, of course, discussing the matter with Christine, I decided to bid on the Boeing 777-200. Subsequently, I was awarded a bid and began training in January 2003. Immediately after starting training, I knew I had made the right decision transitioning to the "Triple Seven." The aircraft was a long- range, wide body, twin-engine jet airliner that could hold more than 300 people. I completed training course and IOE near the end of February. Shortly thereafter, I was presented with a unique opportunity. The United States military was in the process of deploying a large number of military troops to Kuwait in anticipation of a possible invasion into the country of Iraq. During times of a national emergency, when the need for troops to be airlifted exceeds the capacity of available military aircraft, the Department of Defense will call on certain commercial airlines to assist in transporting troops. On March 20, 2003, my crew and I flew to Milan, Italy, where, the next day, we transported a group of soldiers who had arrived from Fort Hood Army Base in Texas on to Kuwait.

While our crew was on layover in Milan, we heard a rumor that the United States and its Allies would be invading Iraq from the country of Kuwait very soon. If there was an invasion, Iraq would retaliate by launching Scud ballistic missiles onto certain targets in Kuwait. When my crew and I reported for duty on March 21, we learned that indeed the invasion of Iraq had commenced during the early hours of that day. Our subsequent departure to Kuwait had to be delayed while U.S. military authorities decided whether it would be safe for us to continue on to Kuwait. During the delay, I had an opportunity to talk with some of the soldiers, both men and women. I was impressed, and very moved at seeing how motivated these soldiers appeared to be—and especially at such a young age. My heart went out to them, and what they were about to face as part of their commitment to serve their country. This was a time of war, and the reality was that there was no guarantee that any of them would return home safely.

For a brief moment my thoughts went back to Steve, a former roommate of mine during my first summer at the Air Force Academy. After graduating from the academy and completing pilot training, Steve, who was only 23 or 24, had been assigned to a fighter aircraft combat unit in South Vietnam when his aircraft was shot down during one of his combat missions.

After a two-hour delay on the ground in Milan, our aircraft was finally released for the flight to Kuwait with instructions to fly there, but land only if conditions were safe. I was also required to check in with Continental Operations every hour to find out if I was cleared to continue on to Kuwait City. Despite some slight disturbances along the way, we were able to deliver the troops and return to Milan without any harm.

A Return Visit to Olla

In the summer of 2003, nearly 50 years after leaving, I made a return visit to Olla. It didn't take long for the memories to come flooding back. Christine and I connected with Jean, my cousin, who drove with us to visit my aunt Leola, Jean's mom, who had moved from Kelly to Columbia. I immediately recognized that beautiful, wide smile when I saw Aunt Leola. I also recalled how that she used to call me "Candy," a nickname that stuck with me for a while. In fact, that's how she referred to me the entire time Christine and I were visiting.

Jean took me to meet Gail, the daughter of my birth father's brother, Jeff Tatum. At first glance, Gail looked at me and exclaimed: "You look just like my daddy!" All the Tatum family members were known for their distinct noses and foreheads. During our visit, she shared about some of the things that had happen in the 50 years since Arnie and I had left Olla, including how her father often spoke of those "two little boys" who moved away.

The next day we drove to Olla. Upon arriving, one of the first buildings I noticed was the old movie theater, which was now abandoned. I stepped out of the car and walked over to the side door that at one time was where blacks entered into the theater. I stood next to the railroad tracks that ran through the center of town. And we drove to the spot where I used to live. My old house had been recently torn down. A block away, tall grass surrounded the old house where I was born. One side of the house itself had collapsed, but the roof remained intact. Between the two houses rested two old, dilapidated shotgun row houses, very similar to the one I once lived in.

Across the street was the house still occupied by my Aunt Rachel, who married Uncle Jeff after we left Olla. Aunt Rachel met us at the front door with a big smile, then gave me a long, hard hug. For the next couple of hours, she talked about the old days, remembering my mother, Charlita; the Tatum family; Uncle Jeff; and other family members. Over the next few days, I spent time with my cousins and other family members, then Christine and I prepared to head back home to Colorado. Now that the visit was over, I was glad to have made the trip back to Olla. It had been a good visit. And I left with a newfound appreciation for my heritage. There were still things I wanted to know about my early life in Louisiana, but I felt I had made a good start during this visit. My time in Louisiana had given me a lot to digest and think about.

A week after my visit to Olla, I went to Fort Worth to see Camille. Since starting work there in 1997, she had moved out of her apartment and bought a new home. She had also bought a new car. She had been working for Kenneth Copeland Ministries for the past six years, and was dating a young man who worked at the ministry's church, Eagle Mountain International Church.

On this visit, Chris invited me to breakfast. It wasn't long before the conversation steered toward the relationship between my daughter and Chris, as he shared how much he loved Camille. Then, in gentlemanly fashion, Chris asked permission to marry my daughter. I had met Chris on a couple of occasions previously, and liked him a lot. The fact that Chris was white, that he was a few years older than Camille, and that he had two children from his previous marriage, may have given me reason for pause many years ago. But over the years, I had learned that being the right person was more than marrying the right person. I felt Camille and Chris were the type of people who would help each other to be the right person for each other.

I responded by telling Chris how much I loved my daughter, and that I always wanted what was best for her. Then, I granted my permission. When we returned from breakfast, Chris asked for Camille's hand in marriage and she accepted. They were married the following October.

Since the middle of 2003, Christine had been traveling monthly to Alabama to help take care of her mother, who was ill. At the beginning of 2004, we decided to move to Philadelphia, where Kym lived. That way, Kym would be able to help take care of her grandmother. The move to Philadelphia meant I would be able to drive to Newark from Philadelphia rather than commute the four hours between Denver and Newark.

In the weeks and months that followed, we faced a number of ups and downs. My friend Rick, who had been diagnosed with cancer some years earlier, passed away in June 2005. That same year, in September, Christine's mother died.

Following her mother's funeral, Christine and I returned home to Philadelphia to face what would be one final momentous chapter in my life: my retirement.

I loved flying, and quite honestly was not ready to give it up. But the choice wasn't mine to make. That decision had been made for me, as Continental's corporate rules and FAA regulations required that all pilots retire at age 60.

I decided that a trip to London would be my retirement flight because London was one of my favorite cities. Ironically, Rick had flown to London on his retirement flight almost five years earlier. With 15 family members and friends wanting to make the flight with me, Christine and I had to work on the logistics of getting them all to Newark and obtaining seats for them on the flights to and from London. We had to secure hotel rooms for the family members in Newark, as well as rooms in London. And there was the matter of planning a retirement party in Newark once we returned from London.

In addition to Christine, the traveling party included Kym, Rick and their three daughters, Morgan, Madison and Mackenzie; Kevin, Christine's son; Corben; Camille, Chris, and their two children, Addison and Alexandra; my brother, Arnie; and my good friends, Othe and Nancy from Atlanta. Othe and Nancy's daughter stayed behind to oversee the preparations for the retirement party, which was to be held at the Newark Wyndham Hotel once we returned. Other family members were scheduled to join us for the party.

The only remaining decisions I needed to make were to choose a first officer to accompany me on the flight, and decide on which day I would fly the aircraft. I chose Chris, a female pilot I had flown with on numerous trips and had come to know and trust. As for which day I would actually fly the aircraft, it needed to be before I actually turned 60 on November 6. FAA rules dictated that a pilot could not fly on his or her actually birthday. I decided to start the trip on Thursday, November 3, and return on Saturday, November 5.

Notices about the retirement party were placed in the Newark pilot and flight attendant crew rooms, inviting them to my retirement party. Christine arranged for a cameraman to record all of my movements on the day of the flight, starting from when I first arrived at the Newark airport. Since the cameraman worked for Continental, he would have access to the aircraft and to the ramp area. The cameraman would not be traveling to London, but he would be recording all the events leading up to and including the aircraft's pushback from the gate in Newark, as well as the events at the retirement party.

On the day of my final flight, I arrived at the Newark airport early to greet the family members and friends who would be making the trip. Later, I went to the Newark flight office to say my goodbye to my assistant flight manager and the base chief pilot. I also met with Chris, my first officer, to review and sign paperwork for the flight. I introduced Chris to our special passengers, who were then allowed to pre-board the plane. Moments later, the base chief pilot came aboard and presented me with a plaque in recognition of my 28-plus years of service to Continental Airlines.

At 7 p.m., the aircraft pushed back from the gate. The engines revved up, and upon receiving clearance from ground control, I maneuvered the giant aircraft into position and taxied out to runway 22 R.

At 7:23 p.m., Continental 18 lifted off and began a 5½-hour flight to London, England.

✈
Flight Log: Approach and Landing

Continental Flight 19 is making its final descent into Newark International Airport. The lead flight attendant has just handed each passenger a copy of a handout that reads as follows:

SALUTE TO YOUR CAPTAIN
Flight 19 London – Newark
November 5, 2005

Continental Airlines, Flight 19 is under the command of Captain Harry Arnold. Federal Aviation regulations mandate an airline pilot's retirement at age 60. This will be Captain's Arnold's final trip as a commercial airline pilot. Captain Arnold has provided Continental Airlines with over 28 years of dedicated aviation service.

Captain Arnold was born in Olla, Louisiana, and grew up in Omaha, Nebraska, where he attended Central High School. Captain Arnold was selected to attend the United States Air Force Academy in Colorado Springs, Colorado. He graduated in 1970 earning a Bachelor of Science degree in Political Science. Captain Arnold was his Class Vice President, Vice-Chairman of the Honor Committee and was selected as the Outstanding Squadron Commander.

Captain Arnold was selected to attend the United States Air Force flight training. He was awarded his Air Force wings in 1971. During his United States Air Force career he flew the T-37B and the C9A. Captain Arnold earned numerous medals, awards and citations for his service with the United States Air Force.

Captain Arnold started his commercial aviation career with Continental Airlines in 1977. During his career with Continental Airlines he has accumulated over 28,000 flying hours. He was specially selected to be a Check Airman Instructor Pilot on the Boeing 737, Boeing 757, Boeing 767 and currently on the Boeing 777. As an Instructor Pilot, he has been responsible for the training, standardization, and proficiency of several hundred pilots during the past several years. During his airline career he has flown the Boeing 727-100/200, Boeing 737-300/500, New Generation Boeing 737-700/800, Boeing 757-200/300, Boeing 767-200/400 and the Boeing 777, on which you are currently flying.

This well-earned retirement will afford Captain Arnold the opportunity to spend quality time with his family and enjoy his hobbies that include: golfing, fishing, tennis and riding his Harley-Davidson.

Traveling with Captain Arnold today is his wife Christine. Also joining him are the Arnolds' children: Camille, Corben, Kym and Kevin with their families including five grandchildren. His brother, Dr. Cornelius Arnold, and family friends Nancy and Othe are also participating in his retirement celebration flight.

Thank you for being a part of Captain's Arnold's final flight at Continental Airlines. Please join us as we salute

Captain Arnold for a 35-year career that has included aviation service to his country and significant aviation contributions to Continental Airlines that have included positions as Check Airman Instructor Pilot and qualification as Pilot-in-Command on every type aircraft in the Continental fleet.

Thank you, Captain Arnold!

The handout was signed by Continental Airlines' Vice President of Flight Operations and the Chief Pilot- New York Flight Operations.

As we proceed to leave the state of New York and enter northern New Jersey, New York Center hands off the flight to New York Approach Control, who gives us a descent to 7,000 feet. The flight will receive radar vectors to mesh in with other Newark inbound flights arriving from the west and south for an approach to runway 22L at Newark.

I have disengaged the auto pilot and am now flying the aircraft. Chris, my first office, chides me by saying, "You better make a good landing because you are going to remember it for a long time."

The heading points the aircraft directly toward New York City.

Now, turn further right to heading 180 degrees for an intercept heading to runway 22 L at Newark.

Approach control is asking if we have the runway in sight. I nod to Chris that we do, and she relays the information to the controller. The approach controller is now clearing us for visual approach to runway 22L and has instructed us to contact Newark tower on frequency 118.3.

The final approach course to runway 22L runs parallel to the Hudson River and to the New York City skyline. On a clear day, passengers seated on the left side of the aircraft get a perfect view of Manhattan Island and the Statue of Liberty. I glance briefly at the skyline for what will be my last view as a pilot flying into Newark.

We are seven miles from the runway threshold and I begin to configure the aircraft for landing. Chris lowers the wing flaps to the approach position. Now five miles from the runway, she lowers the landing gear and I call for a "before landing" checklist.

The Boeing 777 now descends to 1,500 feet above the ground and Chris lowers the wing flaps to landing position. The aircraft is now below 1,000 feet and its automated voice has just come on. The countdown begins: "500, 400, 300, 200, 80, 50, 30, 20...."

As the aircraft passes through 20 feet I begin to slowly reduce the throttles to the idle position, while adding a slight amount of back pressure on the aircraft yoke to slow the aircraft's descent rate for the landing.

"Ten," the countdown continues.

The Boeing 777 has landed!

Although I cannot hear it, I will later be informed that the passengers gave me a loud applause for my landing. After I slow the aircraft to its taxi speed, Chris switches the radio to ground control and tells them that our flight is assigned Gate 131—the same gate from which we departed three days ago. Ground control tells us to taxi to gate 131 via taxiways Delta (D), Bravo (B) and Romeo Echo (RE). As I approached taxiway Romeo Echo, I see two fire trucks on opposite sides of the taxiway. After turning onto taxiway Romeo Echo the aircraft is given a water salute by the firetrucks.

Later, I make a point of thanking the Newark flight office for arranging the water salute because water salutes are usually suspended during the winter months due to the possibility of creating icy spots on the taxiway.

I taxi the aircraft to Gate 131 and shut down the engines. Chris and I then complete the parking checklist. While I was taxiing to the gate, Chris had used the public address system to ask the passengers to remain seated for a few moments after the aircraft was parked at the gate. After completing the "engine shutdown" checklist, I open the flight deck door only to notice the passengers are still seated. At that point, I proceed down the aisle, greeting the passengers and giving them high-fives. When I reach the aft galley of the aircraft, I thank the flight attendants who are working the back portion of the coach section for their help and support. By the time I return to the flight deck all the passengers have deplaned. Chris is still on the flight deck, removing our crew bags.

After retrieving my flight bag and crew bag, I take one last look around the flight deck, turn to Chris and say, "It's time for a party."

Chapter 10

✈

Post-Flight

By the time I arrived at the Newark Customs and Immigrations checkpoint, many of the passengers had already cleared customs. There was a line in customs dedicated specifically to crew members, which allowed me to catch up with my traveling party. As I was leaving the customs area, a young black woman who was on my flight asked if I was one of the first blacks to pilot with Continental. When I replied in the affirmative, she smiled and congratulated me on my retirement. Upon entering the terminal, a loud outburst of cheer broke out from among the traveling party, friends and well-wishers. After checking into our hotel, Christine went immediately to the ballroom to check the status of the retirement party.

At 7 p.m., the master of ceremonies took to the podium, made a few remarks, and directed everyone to the buffet lines. Ron and I had met while going through our initial training on the Boeing 737-300, and had been friends ever since. He had also been a Harley rider along with Rick and me. An hour later, Ron returned to the podium to begin the program. There were three keynote speakers for the evening: Dr. Cornelius Arnold (my brother, Arnie); Captain Reuben Jones, and General Norman Elliott.

Arnie took the liberty of the occasion to speak about our childhood growing up, and kindly titled his little speech, "The Way He Was." Reuben Jones, who was a classmate in the Air Force Academy, shared about our time together in the academy.

He titled his speech, "Cross Into the Blue."

Norman, also a friend from our days at the academy, was perhaps the least brutal (just joking), as he shared about out time together as pilots. His talk was titled, "Work Hard, Fly Right." I could not have been more proud to have had those three speak such kind, gracious words about me, and about our close relationships.

Of course there were others, including family members, who took the opportunity to speak words of kindness and offer me their best wishes. I spoke a few words, thanked everyone for their support throughout the years, and finished by saying how much I would miss everyone. The party ended at 11 p.m. It had been a long day, but one I would remember the rest of my life.

The next morning, my birthday, Christine and I had a relaxing breakfast with family and friends. Afterward, we packed the car for our drive back to West Grove. As I turned onto the New Jersey Turnpike, I took one last look at the Newark Airport through my rear view mirror. My mind was filled with emotions. As I contemplated the next chapter in my life, I recalled the poem that was engraved on a plaque given to me by Rick's sister. In some strange way, High Flight signaled the ending of one chapter in my life, but the beginning of another. Read it. Maybe it will speak to your life, as it has mine.

HIGH FLIGHT

Oh! I have slipped the surly bonds of earth,
And danced the skies on laughter-silvered wings;
Sunward I've climbed, and joined the tumbling mirth
Of sun-split clouds, and done a hundred things
You have not dreamed of—Wheeled and soared and swung
High in the sunlit silence. Hov'ring there
I've chased the shouting wind along, and flung
My eager craft through footless halls of air...

Up, up the long, delirious, burning blue
I've topped the wind-swept heights with easy grace
Where never lark or even eagle flew—
And, while with silent lifting mind I've trod
The high untrespassed sanctity of space,
Put out my hand, and touched the face of God.

— John Gillespie Magee, Jr.
Royal Canadian Air Force
World War II